The Development of Western Civilization

*Narrative Essays in the History of Our Tradition from
Its Origins in Ancient Israel and Greece to the Present*

Edited by Edward W. Fox

*Professor of Modern European History
Cornell University*

THE AGE OF REASON

BY FRANK E. MANUEL

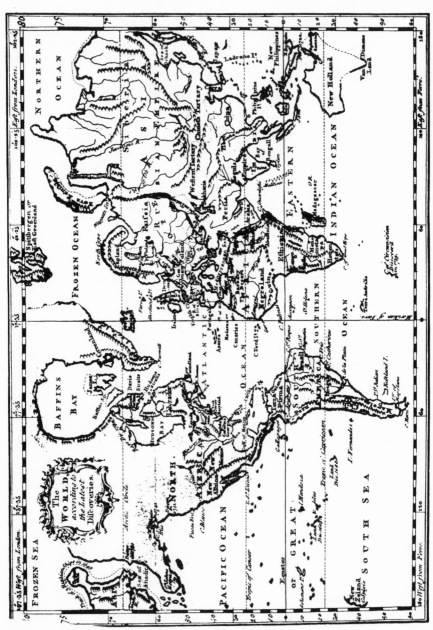

Map of the world, by Thomas Jeffreys, Geographer to His Royal Highness the Prince of Wales, 1760

The Age of Reason

FRANK E. MANUEL

NEW YORK UNIVERSITY

*

GREENWOOD PRESS, PUBLISHERS
WESTPORT, CONNECTICUT

Library of Congress Cataloging in Publication Data

Manuel, Frank Edward.
    The age of reason.

    (The Development of Western civilization)
    Reprint. Originally published: Ithaca : Cornell
University Press, 1951. With new introd.
    Bibliography: p.
    Includes index.
    1. Eighteenth century. 2. Europe--History--18th
century. I. Title. II. Series.
D286.M33 1982   940.2'2   82-2935
ISBN 0-313-23557-0 (lib. bdg.)   AACR2

Reprinted with the permission of Cornell University Press.

Reprinted in 1982 by Greenwood Press,
A division of Congressional Information Service, Inc.
88 Post Road West, Westport, Connecticut 06881

Printed in the United States of America

10 9 8 7 6 5 4 3 2 1

Foreword

THE proposition that each generation must rewrite history is more widely quoted than practiced. In the field of college texts on western civilization, the conventional accounts have been revised, and sources and supplementary materials have been developed; but it is too long a time since the basic narrative has been rewritten to meet the rapidly changing needs of new college generations. In the mid-twentieth century such an account must be brief, well written, and based on unquestioned scholarship and must assume almost no previous historical knowledge on the part of the reader. It must provide a coherent analysis of the development of western civilization and its basic values. It must, in short, constitute a systematic introduction to the collective memory of that tradition which we are being asked to defend. This series of narrative essays was undertaken in an effort to provide such a text for an introductory history survey course and is being published in the present form in the belief that the requirements of that one course reflected a need that is coming to be widely recognized.

Now that the classic languages, the Bible, the great historical novels, even most non-American history, have dropped out of the normal college preparatory program, it is imperative that a text in the history of European civilization be fully self-explanatory. This means not only that it must begin at the beginning, with the origins of our civilization in ancient Israel and Greece, but that it must introduce every name or event that takes an integral place in the account and ruthlessly delete all others no matter how firmly imbedded in historical protocol. Only thus simplified and complete will the narrative present a sufficiently clear outline of those major trends and developments that have led from the beginning of our recorded time to the most pressing of our current problems. This simplification, however, need not involve intellectual dilution or evasion. On the contrary, it can effectively raise rather than lower the level of presentation. It is on this assumption that the present series has been based, and each contributor has been urged to write for a mature and literate audience. It is hoped, therefore, that the essays may also prove profitable and rewarding to readers outside the college classroom.

The plan of the first part of the series is to sketch, in related essays, the narrative of our history from its origins to the eve of the French Revolution; each is to be written by a recognized scholar and is designed to serve as the basic reading for one week in a semester course. The developments of the nineteenth and twentieth centuries will be covered in a succeeding series which will provide the same quantity of reading material for each week of the second semester. This scale of presentation has been adopted in the conviction that any understanding of the central problem of the preservation of the integrity and dignity of the individual human being depends first on an examination of the origins of our tradition in the politics and philosophy of the ancient Greeks and the religion of the ancient Hebrews and then on a relatively more detailed knowledge of its recent development within our industrial urban society.

The decision to devote equal space to twenty-five centuries and to a century and a half was based on the analogy with the human memory. Those events most remote tend to be remembered in least detail but often with a sense of clarity and perspective that is absent in more recent and more crowded recollections. If the roots of our tradition must be identified, their relation to the present must be carefully developed. The nearer the narrative approaches contemporary times, the more difficult and complicated this becomes. Recent experience must be worked over more carefully and in more detail if it is to contribute effectively to an understanding of the contemporary world.

It may be objected that the series attempts too much. The attempt is being made, however, on the assumption that any historical development should be susceptible of meaningful treatment on any scale and in the realization that a very large proportion of today's college students do not have more time to invest in this part of their education. The practical alternative appears to lie between some attempt to create a new brief account of the history of our tradition and the abandonment of any serious effort to communicate the essence of that tradition to all but a handful of our students. It is the conviction of everyone contributing to this series that the second alternative must not be accepted by default.

In a series covering such a vast sweep of time, few scholars would find themselves thoroughly at home in the fields covered by more than one or two of the essays. This means, in practice, that almost every essay should be written by a different author. In spite of apparent drawbacks, this procedure promises real advantages. Each contributor will be in a position to set higher standards of accuracy and insight in an essay encompassing a major portion of the field of his life's work than could ordinarily be expected in surveys of some ten or twenty centuries. The inevitable discontinuity of style and interpretation could be modified by editorial co-ordination; but it was felt that some discontinuity was in itself desirable. No illusion is more easily acquired by the student in an elementary course, or is more prejudicial to the efficacy of such a course, than that a single smoothly articulated text represents the very substance of history itself. If the shift from author to author, week by week, raises difficulties for the beginning student, they are difficulties that will not so much impede his progress as contribute to his growth.

This essay, *The Age of Reason*, by Mr. Frank E. Manuel, is the second of the series to be published. It presents for the beginning student a carefully balanced introduction to both the social background and the intellectual achievements of the eighteenth century. Though this period has long been studied as a source of many of our basic political assumptions, it has tended to remain one of the least understood chapters of our past. The very familiarity of its intellectual climate has tended to divert attention from the fact that its material way of life was almost as different from ours today as was that of Thomas Aquinas or even Julius Caesar. Nor is the difficulty of comprehending the differences between Voltaire's day and ours a problem only for the classroom. To an important extent it is failure to reconcile the dictates of the political convictions inherited from the eighteenth century with the necessities of the industrial society bequeathed by the nineteenth that has made the twentieth century such a bewildering epoch in which to live. It is hardly necessary to urge, therefore, that the subject of this essay illustrates to an unusual degree the proposition—on which the entire series is based—that an accurate appreciation of the past is necessary to an effective understanding of the present.

Both author and editor wish to express their gratitude to Mr. Leo Gershoy and Mr. Crane Brinton for their many helpful suggestions.

EDWARD WHITING FOX

Ithaca, New York
October, 1950

Contents

Foreword, by Edward Whiting Fox   v

Prolegomena   1

I   The European World   8

II   Science and Theology   23

III   The Moral and Political Outlook   35

IV   The Realm of France   49

V   The British System   69

VI   Empire of the Hapsburgs   86

VII   Prussia: The State as Machine   99

VIII   Russia: The Servile State   106

IX   Balance of Power in War and Peace   113

Chronological Summary   137

Suggestions for Further Reading   139

Index   143

THE AGE OF REASON

Prolegomena

THE Age of Reason is not merely a convenient catch phrase coined by modern historians to characterize the period from the Peace of Utrecht (1713) to the French Revolution of 1789. During the course of the eighteenth century itself, the kings and ministers who ruled the European states, as well as the intellectuals and writers who dominated public opinion, were keenly aware of the unique quality of their epoch. They themselves earnestly believed that they were living in an age of reason, a century of enlightenment, the dawn of a new era of civilization and progress.

For it was a period when reason virtually replaced religion as the guiding principle in art, thought, and the governance of men. Among intellectuals, ideas and institutions ceased to be respected simply because they were based on tradition, precedent, religious dogma, and authority. Unquestioned acceptance of the old order of society and the old ways of statecraft yielded to a new spirit of critical inquiry which demanded some rational justification for the existing social system. Men asked forthrightly whether their laws and customs enhanced or diminished the wealth of nations and the happiness of peoples.

The general application of reason, it was thought, would

emancipate Europe from the artificialities, restrictions, injustices, and superstitions which had been inherited from the "Dark Ages" and which served only to impede progress. Reason would create a society of law and order, a smooth-running mechanism whose consistency and harmony would mirror the workings of the natural universe.

The status occupied by the feudal aristocracy and the higher clergy of the official churches of Europe constituted the chief obstacle to the transformation of society. The traditions, customs, and autonomous rights of the nobility and the church were essentially alien to the spirit of rationalism and operated to block the establishment of centralized, well-ordered states. At this stage in the historical development of Europe few men wanted the complete eradication of these privileged estates; the ideals of the age could be realized by curbing rather than eliminating the favored social orders.

In central and eastern Europe and many minor states of the continent, the principal contenders against the powers of the nobility and the clergy were the dynastic sovereigns. Competition among the great states was ruthless and the monarchy which failed to overhaul its internal administration faced dismemberment. Seeking to consolidate their own authority the crowned heads wrestled with the separatism of provinces which their royal houses had inherited through mediaeval and seventeenth-century wars and marriages. They tried to introduce uniformity in law and administration throughout their realms and to smash the opposition of nobles and clerics fighting to retain their prerogatives to tax, govern, and dispense justice. The very direction of foreign policy was at stake, because there were aristocracies who attempted to reassert their independence to the point of deciding for themselves upon issues of war and peace. The administrative reforms of the century were promulgated by royal edict without the consent of and often despite such representative diets and assemblies as had survived from the Middle Ages to become fortresses of aristocratic reaction.

Frederick II of Prussia, Joseph II of Austria, and Catherine II of Russia were for the intellectuals of the second half of the century embodiments of an ideal of monarchical government which has been called enlightened despotism. What they had in common essentially was a passion and a need for centralization, unification, and rationalization in government. Because it was in harmony with their own drive toward centralism, the despots accepted the belief of the intellectuals of the age that feudal practices were not compatible with reason, justice, and natural law.

The enlightened despots used different tactics, but their purpose was always the same: to integrate the aristocracy with the machinery of the state and to establish the absolute sovereignty of the dynastic monarch over them. The force of the nobility was far from spent in eighteenth-century Europe and their support of the central government often had to be bought with material rewards and blandishments. In Prussia and Russia the compliance of the nobility was paid for by the extension rather than the weakening of their hold over peasants and serfs. Despite the accumulated wealth and power of the church, it was ordinarily the easier of the privileged orders to deal with, and even where aristocratic resistance was most obstinate, the subservience of the clergy to the monarchy was finally established.

In the three continental powers of central and eastern Europe, new and detailed systems of governmental administration were drafted. There was a tendency to soften the cruel punishments of the past. In theory, if not always in practice, legal codes and a great judicial structure built on uniform procedures granted the people a measure of protection both from harsh customary rules and from the rough justice of local lords. The mere issuance by a royal commission of new codes of written law did not automatically bring more equitable administration of justice to those of low estate, since in many instances the same nobles who had once been responsible for the enforcement of the customary law were called upon to interpret the new codes. But at least the royal decrees set up a standard and acted as a checkrein upon magistrates who had formerly heeded only the confusing dictates of custom and the promptings of caprice.

In order to adapt their administrative systems to a growing centralism, the enlightened despots made a bureaucratic revolution. They altered the basic character of government by creating special departments and agencies whose jurisdiction was kingdom-wide. Their officials made tours, wrote reports, and saw to it that orders were transmitted to all parts of the realm. Governmental decrees were interpreted logically and consistently, and any departure from rules required a special justification. Bureaucracy became a guardian against the arbitrary use of power not only on the part of local lords but even by the crown itself. A monarch could hardly exercise his whim often enough to modify seriously the effect of daily decisions by his army of civil servants. As David Hume, the Scottish philosopher and historian, reflected, among the galaxy of absolute princes in Europe there were no tyrants cast in the mold of Caligula or Nero. "It may now be affirm'd of civiliz'd Monarchies, what was formerly said in Praise of Republics alone, *that they are a Government of Laws, not of men.* They are found susceptible of Order, Method, and Constancy, to a surprising Degree." [1]

The innovations of the enlightened despots should not be confused with democratic reforms. In revamping the administrative machinery of their states, the autocrats were not moved by consideration for the human rights of their subjects so much as they were by their own exigencies. Whatever benefits accrued to individual peasant or *bourgeois* in the process of state reorganization were usually incidental to the final purposes of despotism in war against the aristocracy and in war against a rival dynasty. Indeed, the attempt to replace "irrational" customary law and its tribunals with a system of orders handed down by the monarch and based on the paramount interest or "reason" of the centralized dynastic state could and often did create a tyranny of its own. A multiplicity of regulations, many of them absurd with minutiae, were poured forth to order every kind of human relationship.

In central and eastern Europe the underlying conflict remained the tug of war between the monarchy and the aristocracy, since there was no middle class of merchants, manufacturers, and professional men substantial enough to challenge the position of the nobles. The *bourgeois* was under royal patronage, not an aggressive force in his own right.

In Britain and France it was the middle classes, directors of new productive enterprise and commerce, who were the active enemies of "irrational" feudal residues which impeded free movement and progress. The *bourgeoisie* of the West

[1] David Hume, *Essays Moral and Political* (London, 1741–1742), I, 283–284.

identified the growth of their own prosperity and power with reason. By 1750 the realignment of the old and the new forces in British and French society was already far advanced. Britain had undergone a "Great Rebellion" and a "Glorious Revolution" in the seventeenth century, the first in Christian Europe, and had emerged with a new constitution protecting commercial interests and providing for their representation in the government of the nation. In the course of the eighteenth century the integration and working compromise of the English aristocracy and merchant class proceeded apace, accompanied by no more dramatic clash than the election contests of Tories and Whigs. In France, the Bourbon monarchy had already produced in the seventeenth century its great autocrat, Louis XIV, who had curbed the power of the nobility and imposed upon the state a centralized, bureaucratic mechanism, one which was subsequently imitated by the enlightened despots of the rest of the continent. But the absolute monarchy under Louis XIV's successors failed to amalgamate the nobility and the *bourgeoisie*, and toward the end of the century the rivalry of these two classes was sharply accentuated until it flared forth in civil war—the great French Revolution.

Wherever men—kings or commoners—set themselves in opposition to the old order, they were applauded by the intellectuals of Europe. The *philosophes*, or popular philosophers, who were overwhelmingly commoners in origin, smarted under the humiliating restraints and disabilities imposed by the aristocrats. Even more bitterly than they assaulted the position of the nobility, the *philosophes* attacked the Christian churches which had thrown the protective mantle of religion about the iniquities of society. The intellectuals used the discoveries and the methods of science to refute and to mock the teachings of mediaeval Christianity. They turned the attention of their contemporaries to the pursuit of happiness in this world, and tried to emancipate them both from fear of the church and respect for the aristocracy.

In reorganizing their states the monarchs were impelled not only by a desire to dominate the nobility, but by the need to build formidable military machines based on effective government. Even when the enlightened despots befriended the men of learning and talked the language of the most advanced thinkers of their day, their major preoccupations remained war and territorial aggrandizement. The whole history of the eighteenth century could be written in terms of a struggle for power among dynastic states on the European continent and in the colonies. Battles were fought intermittently throughout the century, and by the eve of the French Revolution the European states system as formulated at the Peace of Utrecht had undergone rather important alterations. The traditional diplomatic alignment of Bourbon *versus* Hapsburg had been upset by the rise of Russia and Prussia. These two states of eastern Europe had emerged as nations of great potential power; the impact of their dynamic expansionism was first felt in this period. In the colonial world the outcome of a century of sporadic warfare was decisive. France was virtually ousted from the continents of Asia and America, and England—ruled by the men of industry and trade—became the preponderant maritime and colonial power.

CHAPTER I

The European World ~~~~~~~

EIGHTEENTH-CENTURY world maps furnished Europeans with a reasonably accurate impression of the coastal outlines of the great continents and islands, except for a strangely shaped New Holland (Australia) and a totally unexplored American Northwest. Of the several continents, Europe proper was the only one whose settlements had been extensively charted. Detailed maps for all its political subdivisions had been prepared by learned societies and army staffs in order to guide generals in their military operations and to facilitate the policing of the state. In other parts of the world, little beyond the coastal fringe where the major colonial factories, seaports, and fortified places were located had been accurately surveyed.

Although to most Europeans the interior of these continents remained dark and mysterious, the frontiers of geographic knowledge continued to recede. Explorers, traders, and colonists pushed their way up the river valleys of North America, charted islands in the South Pacific, established new posts on the West African coast and on the rivers of India. A profusion of exotic voyage literature was avidly devoured by those who stayed at home.

Europe itself consisted of some two hundred separate political units, dependent in varying degree upon the major powers and ruled by a Holy Roman Emperor and a bewildering array of tsars, kings, princes, dukes, bishops, electors, and city administrators. Cartographers continued to use "Germany" and "Italy" as geographic expressions, although they identified no united political entities. Vestiges of complex feudal relationships existed among the reigning houses of Europe. Chancelleries of states great and small were well stocked with mediaeval charters which awarded their monarchs conflicting suzerainties in one another's lands. When questions of royal succession shook the delicate balance of power there were ample precedents and documentary justifications for a pretender's claims. No king was ever wanting a *casus belli*. Maps generally indicated the actualities of power relationships on the continent as defined by treaties; if the sonorous titles of European monarchs had ever been represented graphically, the result would have been a crazy quilt of overlapping boundaries.

Growth of Population

In the eighteenth century no one knew what the population of Europe was. In addition to the administrative difficulties inherent in conducting a census, governments were deterred by the prevalent superstition that it was evil to count human souls, as well as by the simple political consideration that the size of a nation-state's population was a treasured military secret, for it indicated the man power which would be available in time of war. Contemporary taxation and army conscription tables in a few countries nonetheless do give some idea of numbers. In recent years estimates of past population growth have been compiled on the basis of such old records, and while the demographers are apologetic about the high percentage of error involved in their calculations, the figures at least indicate general magnitudes for the century.

In 1650, we now believe, the population of Europe was about 100,000,000. During the following hundred years there was an increase of 40,000,000, raising the total to 140,-000,000 in 1750. In the course of the second half of the eighteenth century occurred the first sharp acceleration of population growth in modern times, a jump to 187,000,000 by 1800. This was largely the consequence of a decline in the death rate, it is supposed, and not of any extraordinary increase in fertility. It may be of interest to set these figures beside the even more hazardous conjectures about the movement of population in Asia, which rose from 330,000,000 to 600,000,000 during the same period. Thus by the year 1800 the number of human beings in the whole world was approaching 1,000,000,000, about a fifth of whom were white Europeans in origin, living on their own continent and in the colonies.

The spectacular growth of the latter half of the eighteenth century was a novel phenomenon the like of which had not occurred in Europe since the Middle Ages. Of itself, the impact of this sudden multiplication of persons inhabiting a small area of the world, the European peninsula, was forceful enough to disrupt stable relationships in many spheres of economic and political activity.

A few rough estimates will indicate the relative population weights among the major states at the close of the century. France was preponderant in western Europe, by far the largest single nation-state, with a population of 24,-000,000. England and Wales were still under 10,000,000, and Prussia under 5,000,000. The combined state areas of

Austria and Hungary had only about 8,000,000, though the dispersed pieces of their whole continental empire gave the Hapsburg rulers access to total man power comparable to that of the French monarchy. The vast unexplored frontier of Russia in Asia makes it impossible to rely on any single number for that empire. In 1797 a figure as high as 36,000,000 was used in an official registry of persons on crown and noble lands. Other contemporary estimates, restricted to those portions of Russia which could effectively bear weight in the European balance of power, ran as low as 9,000,000. Farsighted calculators were already aware of the military importance of this enormous reservoir of population reaching to the Pacific.

The Movement to the Cities

In the late seventeenth and early eighteenth centuries, a group of "political arithmeticians" in England, France, and Germany undertook the first studies of what we would now call vital statistics. They discovered that in the cities of Europe they had sampled, the annual number of births fell below deaths. Consequently, they reasoned, had there been no migration from rural to urban areas, the cities would be suffering a steady population decline. Since it was a commonplace of observation that, contrariwise, towns were increasing in size, they could not but conclude that the cities were in fact attracting a regular flow of persons from the countryside large enough to more than compensate for the natural loss. Thus, without any positive statistical proof of population movement to the city, they deduced it from their analysis of burial and baptismal records. Despite the "fetid atmosphere" of the eighteenth-century town, the ravages of disease in congested quarters, the weakness of man's "vital forces" in the city, and the evils of debauchery, the early statisticians reported that men and women continued to be drawn to these centers of vice and luxury, abandoning the soil with its "constant, parsimonious, and contented inhabitants."

In England, where the development was most striking, the growth of the city was the consequence of both industrial and agricultural revolutions, the allurement of urban luxury based on commercial prosperity, the increased employment opportunities for artisans, maids, and lackeys, and the improvement of the transportation system, which made the escape to London town a somewhat less perilous undertaking. The speeding-up of the enclosure movement sent into the cities rural agricultural workers and cottagers whose labor was not required for the farming of consolidated estates. During the course of the eighteenth century the independent yeomen of ancient England began to disappear. They were either bought out by the new rich merchant class who had gone to the country to accumulate landed property for respectability's sake, or they were forced out when their commons were enclosed by the Whig gentry who seized the land through manipulation of the procedures of local justice and through acts of Parliament. Bought out or driven out, the yeomen and agricultural laborers became industrial entrepreneurs, workers, or servants in urban areas. As the industrial revolution got well under way in the second half of the century, whole areas of England witnessed a new concentration of population, especially the textile centers of Lancashire and West Riding, the pottery centers of Staffordshire and Warwickshire, and the coal fields of Durham and Northumberland. There seems to have been a general shift of population from the south and the southeast to the midlands and the north. By 1801 England and Wales were by far the most urbanized areas in Europe; together they had more than a hundred cities and towns, each with a population of 5,000 or over, and these "urban" agglomerations accounted for 2,300,000 inhabitants out of a total of about 8,900,000.

Throughout the century the continent of Europe remained overwhelmingly rural. In France the urban movement was far less intense than in England. The peasantry was attached to its native soil, though the rising demand in Paris for artisans and servants and, on a lesser scale, the attractions of the flourishing and expanding commercial cities of the provinces drew the foot-loose and the adventurous. There are no precise statistical data for each city, but the rapid eighteenth-century growth of Nantes, Marseilles, Nancy, Lyons, Bordeaux, and Le Havre is shown by the number of buildings which have survived from that epoch. French textile centers in the northern provinces also expanded, although the concentration of workers was at no time comparable to the English factory towns. By 1800 France had ninety cities with a population of more than 10,000, which accounted for at least 10 per cent of the total population. In rather turgid moralistic excursions, a number of contemporary French economists deplored the abandonment of the countryside where, they believed, the nation's true prosperity lay in the treasures of the earth. Most physiocrats, as this school was called, denounced urban luxury as destructive of the national wealth. The political philosopher and writer, Jean-Jacques Rousseau (1712–1778), with more style and passion, joined in bewailing the loss of the simple virtues of natural man in the corruption of the city. The countrymen nevertheless did not cease their steady trek to the towns.

Germany remained predominantly rural and poor. It has been estimated that at the end of the century only a fourth of the inhabitants lived in agglomerations of more than a thousand persons. The numerous German ducal courts which aped the splendour of Versailles were tiny establishments located in what would now be considered mere towns. The Weimar of Goethe's day had about 8,000 inhabitants.

As one moved east across the European continent the urban units became smaller and rarer until they vanished in the Russian steppe.

The Capitals of Europe

Among the cities of Europe, there were some hundred magnificent islands of urban culture on which massive stone structures had been raised by successive centuries of Christian civilization. About a dozen of these larger cities had achieved eminence as the capitals of great states and empires. From these few cities the rulers of men ordered the destinies of a continent still overwhelmingly agricultural.

Contemporary city plans and guidebooks have left us a fair notion of the dimensions and population density of the major cities, symbols of the wealth and prosperity of the European nations.

The outstanding metropolis was London, eighteen miles in circumference and inhabited by nearly 900,000 persons. "No City can boast of more Conveniences," wrote an Englishman proudly in 1771:

It is encompassed with a vast Number of Fruit and Kitchen Gardens; for many Miles there are Roads to it, kept in constant

Repair; every House almost is supplied with Water by Pipes from the Thames, and New-River, or the Ponds at Hampstead. There is in every Street, a Common-Sewer to carry off the Filth; and when the Pavement is finished, which is now in very great Forwardness, there will be no Town better paved and lighted.[1]

Paris was estimated at 700,000 persons, crowded into four-to-seven-story houses along a thousand crooked streets. The circuit of Rome was nominally ten miles around, but half the area, where noble edifices had once stood, was now returned to wasteland and open fields. Amsterdam, though it had lost its trade supremacy to the overseas companies of London, was still a banking center with 200,000 inhabitants. Vienna, seat of the Hapsburg Empire and long the last outpost of European civilization, was primarily a bureaucratic center, no more populous than the Dutch capital. The Russians had two capitals: ancient Moscow, with its 1,600 churches and 150,000 people, and new St. Petersburg, constructed on a rational plan with broad straight streets— Peter the Great's "window to the west," which was fast developing also as a key trading mart for the Far East. Constantinople, the capital which the Turks had wrested from the Byzantine Empire, was the equal in size of any in Europe. Berlin was the fastest-growing capital on the continent; it more than trebled its population in the course of the century, attaining about 180,000 in 1800, a barometer of the astounding growth of the new Prussian monarchy. The free cities of Germany, the capitals of the electorates of the

[1] John Andrews, *A Collection of Plans of the Most Capital Cities of Every Empire, Kingdom, Republic and Electorate in Europe and Some Remarkable Cities in the Other Three Parts of the World, with a Description of Their Most Remarkable Buildings, Trade, Situation, Extent, Etc., etc.* (London, 1771), pp. 1-2.

Holy Roman Empire, and the Italian cities of Renaissance grandeur were no longer expanding significantly; they had fallen behind the nation-states and empires.

The cities of Europe included within their boundaries an imposing array of establishments—repositories of their civilization, agencies of domination, institutions for charity and entertainment. There were customhouses, courts, asylums, hospitals, museums of antiquities and curiosities, shops, markets, palaces, arsenals, opera houses, theatres, colleges, libraries, jails, and churches. In tolerant London, Amsterdam, Berlin, and Moscow, there were churches of many denominations; the true church alone could raise its cross in Rome, Paris, and Vienna. For all this resplendence, world travelers reported that the European cities could hardly equal the ancient Chinese capital of Peking with its 2,000,000 inhabitants and scores of shining palaces.

The Rulers of Men

In the great realms of Europe, millions of subjects lived out their mature years knowing only a single monarch. England was ruled by three Georges of Hanover in direct succession, father to son, for more than a hundred years following 1714. Of the Bourbons of France, Louis XV reigned for almost half a century after 1715 and Louis XVI held his throne until deprived of it by the revolutionaries. The domination of Maria Theresa over the Hapsburg possessions lasted from 1740 to 1780; her son Joseph II became a participant in power in 1765 when he was crowned Holy Roman Emperor, and after her demise he governed alone until 1790. In Prussia two Hohenzollerns with intense fixity of purpose, though opposites in character, encompass almost the whole century: Frederick William I ruled from 1713 to 1740, his son Frederick II, known as the Great, until 1786. After Peter the Great's death in 1725 and a rapid succession of minor tsars and tsarinas, the Romanov empire became the heritage of two women, Elizabeth from 1741 to 1762 and Catherine II from 1762 to 1796. Monarchs who endure so long must leave their imprint, for good or evil, upon the state.

The great ministers had briefer tenures in office for sundry reasons, ranging from the vicissitudes of party government in England to the inconstancy of a tsarina's affections in Russia. But in the realm of France figures like Cardinal Fleury (1653–1743) and the Duc de Choiseul (1719–1785), and in Austria Count Haugwitz (1700–1765) and the Prince von Kaunitz (1711–1794), played such dominant roles in shaping governmental policies that, though subjects of the monarch, they were hardly his servants. In a number of the minor European states, the crowned head became little more than a Merovingian puppet, manipulated by a wily expert in statecraft and in the art of dominating superiors in status. The regime of the "Portuguese Richelieu," the Marquis de Pombal (1699–1782), is the most striking example of this ministerial dictatorship. The royal mistresses of Europe, many of them endowed with far greater longevity than is the normal fate in their profession, exerted power in a few of the petty courts of Europe and in France during the reign of Louis XV; in the other great realms monarchy was not, in fact, unduly subject to the influence of the bedchamber.

Princes of the blood and great nobles, at the apex of the social pyramid, were members of a glamorous international aristocracy. As a result of marriage or death, they were called upon to govern one or another of the continental states as

monarchs by divine right or to rule as vassals over one of
the many picayune principalities into which German- and
Italian-speaking lands had been chopped up. Despite language difficulties, monarchs shifted nationality with relative
ease when royal succession called them to foreign thrones.
Catherine II of Russia was a German princess, and the
Georges of England were Hanoverians.

Travelers, Migrants, Exiles

Men began to travel more frequently as the centralized
states of Europe constructed better highways to ride on and
made them safer from brigandage. Noble Englishmen's sons
and their tutors took the Grand Tour and dashed through
the capitals of the continent. An impoverished poet like
Oliver Goldsmith (1728–1774) made his way in more humble fashion, playing his flute for his supper in peasant huts.
Russians appeared in Paris; the *philosophes* Diderot (1713–
1784) and Grimm (1723–1807) braved the Russian snows
to visit Catherine II; Voltaire (1694–1778) accepted the
hospitality of Frederick II in Berlin; French writers crossed
the Channel to admire English liberties; English philosophers
journeyed to France and Switzerland; the young Goethe
(1749–1832) was dazzled by the beauties of Italy. The man
of letters, like the military commander of parts, was made
at home in any one of the enlightened courts of the continent. The intermittent wars of the century did not significantly impede the movement of persons across state
boundaries, and since war was usually restricted to the battlefield, an enemy alien was not necessarily suspect nor did
he run any great risk of forfeiting his life or his liberty. Monarchs themselves traveled, and when they visited other countries they did not restrict themselves to polite conversation
at the royal courts, but sought out artisans and manufactur-

ers at work and studied experimental farming. Students from Russia were sent to the more advanced countries of the west to learn the newest agricultural methods—a dubious personal opportunity; for, as the British agriculturist and traveler Arthur Young (1741–1820) reports, they were fearful lest failure to comprehend the novelties bring exile to Siberia as punishment for their obtuseness. There were voluntary expatriates who established colonies in each other's countries and taught foreign languages. The French teacher, male and female, appeared as a fixture of genteel society throughout Europe. Great adventurers made their entrances and exits leaving havoc in their train. It was the age of Casanova the lover (1725–1798) and of Cagliostro the magician and impostor (1743–1795).

Apart from these individual wanderings, there were mass migrations on an international scale whose volume it is difficult to estimate. Perhaps as many as a million persons, including transported criminals, sailed from England for the colonies during the century. A steady migration to England from across the Irish Sea was accentuated during the famine of 1782–1784. In 1750 about 100,000 Serbs, angered by Hapsburg decrees which subjected them to Hungarian rule, passed across the border into Russia. And there was an irregular movement of artisans defying national boundaries, even though most European states enforced police restrictions on their emigration in order to protect the supply of laborers in time of peace and of recruits for the army in time of war. England was especially worried about the foreigner's enticement of skilled artisans who might bear away with them treasured industrial secrets, and in 1782 a law was passed prohibiting their emigration. Nevertheless a small number of skilled artisans from industrially advanced England continued to find their way to France by clandestine means. From France in turn there was a trickle to other parts of Europe. These men became agents in the diffusion of the new technology.

The only great religious expulsion of the century struck the Jesuits, who were driven from Portugal, Spain, Austria, and France, seats of their former power, and were, ironically enough, received by the atheistical king of Prussia. Occasionally a philosopher or a writer was banished from one of the Catholic countries for his heretical pronouncements, only to be hailed in triumph in a neighboring land.

Jews, traditional victims of mass expulsions in Europe, were allowed to remain at peace in those states where they had infiltrated, though they continued to suffer disabilities. Catherine II of Russia (1729–1796), however, did establish a limit to their penetration eastward into her territory. In the eighteenth century the trend of Jewish migration from west to east began to reverse itself: a few stray Jews moved from the ghettoes of Poland into the urban centers of Germany and Holland, where they hoped to enjoy the tranquillity of western European tolerance and enlightenment; others ventured as far as Bordeaux.

A European Consciousness

Improved facilities for travel and the relatively easy exchange of ideas helped to develop among the upper classes a European consciousness. The term "cosmopolitan" had a positive connotation in literate eighteenth-century circles, and cosmopolitan meant European. The intellectuals often referred to themselves as Europeans and were aware that the Enlightenment was a European movement sweeping through all the nations of the continent. However, the formal culture and manners of one nation, France, tended to impose themselves upon all others, and stamped the Age of Reason with a Gallic imprint. French was the common international language of intellectual converse as well as of diplomacy, and the "Europeans" and "Cosmopolites" looked to Paris as their capital.

Simultaneously with the spread of a European consciousness there was a literary renascence which gave expression to the national spirit and national patriotism of many individual European peoples. But modern nationalism was not a powerful ideological force before the French Revolution and Napoleon. Romantic nationalism—the idea of the unique genius and superiority of the Englishman, Frenchman, German, Russian, or Spaniard—was an intellectual tendency which, though it had its roots in the eighteenth century, flowered extravagantly only in the nineteenth.

As far as the great mass of the peasants were concerned, they were hardly touched by a profound national consciousness, and surely not by any awareness of themselves as Europeans. They knew that they were Christian and they were bound by their familial and local loyalties. They lived out their lives without venturing further than a few miles from their birthplace and their emotional horizon was geographically limited. Territorial transfers effected by the powers in wartime did not move the peasants deeply as long as their huts escaped the firebrands of enemy troops.

The next two chapters present the main currents of new ideas which coursed through the European continent and the strip of territory inhabited by British colonials in America. Although the ideas were not shared by the mass of the people and the traditionalists among the ruling classes, it was precisely these novel conceptions of the intellectual innovators which marked the Age of Reason with its distinctive character.

CHAPTER II

Science and Theology ⁓⁓⁓⁓⁓⁓

ISAAC NEWTON (1642–1727) had synthesized the heritage of the sixteenth and the seventeenth centuries in physics, astronomy, mathematics, and mechanics, and had added to them his own epoch-making discoveries. The whole formed a compact body of laws explaining the physical universe which was more convincing than any previous scientific synthesis attempted by man. Not many Europeans were erudite enough to comprehend his *Philosophiae Naturalis Principia Mathematica* (1687) in the original Latin, but in a popularized form this vision of the world had a tremendous impact upon men's minds in the succeeding centuries. The vogue for simplified expositions even called forth a special *Newtonism for the Ladies* in Italian.

The reading public of Europe lost interest in theological disputations about religious dogma as they became absorbed in contemplation of Newton's world-machine, whose rules of motion both of celestial bodies in the heavens and of objects on earth were translated into mathematical formulae. It was amazing to realize that the whole universe was subject to identical physical laws and that these laws could be expressed in mathematical symbols which no one could deny or about which there could be no substantial difference of opinion. Even the skeptical David Hume (1711-1776) expressed his wonderment at the perfect functioning of this world-machine, subdivided into an infinite number of lesser machines: "All these various machines, and even their most minute parts, are adjusted to each other with an accuracy, which ravishes into admiration all men, who have ever contemplated them." [1]

Science and Sectarian Theology

The theologians of the various Christian churches had always been divided among themselves. The new science gave men a sense of security and finitude because it seemed to produce incontrovertible propositions which would stand impregnable for all time. "Every sect, in whatever sphere, is the rallying-point for doubt and error. Scotist, Thomist, Realist, Nominalist, Papist, Calvinist, Molinist, and Jansenist are only pseudonyms. There are no sects in geometry. . . ." [2] wrote Voltaire in his *Philosophical Dictionary*. Two scientists in different parts of the world, Newton in England and Leibnitz (1646–1716) in Germany, had simultaneously discovered the calculus through independent ratiocination. Few men dared contradict the Newtonian system once it was published. When an advance was made in physics or mathematics it achieved the status of a generally recognized truth about the world which anyone who had studied the elementary principles of these sciences could comprehend. The theologians of the various Christian sects were eternally denying one another's premises, proving one

---

[1] David Hume, *Dialogues Concerning Natural Religion*, 2d ed. (London, 1779), p. 47.

[2] *Voltaire's Philosophical Dictionary*, sel. and tr. by H. I. Woolf (New York, 1924), p. 267.

another's affirmations to be falsehoods, denouncing one another as heretics. The suspicion soon dawned upon inquiring minds that either these theological quibblings were a pack of nonsense, or that they concerned themselves with matters which could not be fathomed and therefore ought to be let alone, or that they were rousing men to shed one another's blood over issues which were intrinsically of no consequence. Science was yielding a regular harvest of new discoveries in every field. Why repeat arguments about theology which were usually circular, were of no avail, never reached a widely accepted conclusion, and only ended in civil wars, massacres, and burnings at the stake?

Science as practiced in the laboratory of the physicist Robert Boyle (1627–1691) or as propounded in the writings of Newton did not in and of itself solve the problems of man's destiny on earth or the mystery of creation. Indeed, many of the fathers of seventeenth-century science accepted traditional religious dogmas along with their scientific view of the physical world after creation. Newton himself was profoundly religious and he wrote a commentary on the Book of Daniel. Some proceeded with their researches and experiments as if the two worlds of science and theology were quite separate and distinct. Many of them acted from conviction; others merely gave lip service to revealed religion to keep out of trouble with the authorities.

Science, however, was steadfastly undermining the Christian view of the world even though the scientists did not attack the church frontally, continued to render it formal obedience, and received its sacraments. Science as a form of knowledge deflected interest from a striving to comprehend the nature of God and his relationship to man to nonmetaphysical researches which were discovering new laws for the physical universe. The external world became the focus of intellectual interest. Of course there were scientists and laymen who interpreted these laws of nature as the work of Nature's God, men for whom every scientific law was but another proof of the perfect wisdom of God who had created so wonderful a world mechanism. To them, the revelation that the whole universe was subject to an identical set of laws governing motion and gravity served to point up the essential unity of the divine creation. But once they accepted God as an Original Creator or a Prime Mover the scientists did not have further need for His intervention into the workings of the laws of the universe which were destined to go on functioning in the same way forever. Men inevitably became ever more absorbed in uncovering these secret and rational laws of nature and less and less in the God who had created them. Mediaeval thought had considered excessive preoccupation with any aspect of the physical universe evil because the external world could only be a source of sin. The eighteenth century reversed the emphasis and many intellectuals looked askance upon metaphysical questions as a likely way to fall into nonsense, which in the language of the age was equivalent to evil.

Scientific Method Applied to Religion

While scientists in their laboratories and mathematicians in their studies did not engage in open warfare with revealed religion, in eighteenth-century France there arose a group of popular philosophers who took it upon themselves to do battle with the church and to proclaim the conflict between science and religion in a truculent manner. With a few exceptions, these *philosophes* were not scientists themselves. They were rather popularizers and transmitters to the literate public of Europe of the scientific ideas of the seventeenth century, primarily those of Isaac Newton, René Descartes (1596–1650), John Locke (1632–1704), and Francis Bacon (1561–1626). Voltaire was the most brilliant wit in the group, and Denis Diderot the man with the greatest capacity to co-ordinate and simplify for a vast body of readers the scientific knowledge of the age. The *Grande Encyclo-*

Vignette from the *Grande Encyclopédie*, edited by
Denis Diderot and Jean d'Alembert, 1778 edition

pédie, edited by Diderot and Jean d'Alembert (1717–1783) and published from 1751 to 1772, was the great common enterprise in which, despite individual differences, all the philosophers co-operated to present Europe with a unified body of knowledge in the new spirit.

These *philosophes* set up criteria for determining truth which by the end of the century were generally accepted by men outside the church. They allowed as truth only those facts and theories which could be arrived at by the employment of a strict rationalist or scientific method. Their basic principles they adopted from two thinkers of the previous age, Descartes and Bacon, both of whom they assimilated despite fundamental divergences between them. The *phi-losophes* had an oversimplified formulation of the method of science, one hardly adequate in our own day, but it served their purpose.

Descartes had taught them to reason, to deduce knowledge by logical steps from clear and distinct ideas, the best example of which was mathematics. If in any field of knowledge a man could reason from one axiom to another with the certainty of a mathematical demonstration, he was on absolutely secure ground and nobody could doubt his assertions. His original axioms naturally had to be as well founded as his later deductions. "We think," explained Diderot, "that the greatest service to be done to men is to teach them to use their reason, only to hold for truth what they have verified and proved." [3]

Now it was perfectly clear to an eighteenth-century intellectual that theological propositions as well as many of the theories about the origin of kingship were not derived in accordance with the principles of the Cartesian method. While the Christian apologists *appeared* to reason logically from basic premises, they were continually allowing arguments drawn from authority and tradition as embodied in the Bible and other sacred writings to be intermingled with their presentations. Moreover, the primary characteristic of the mathematical spirit, as the *philosophes* understood it, was its emphasis on consistency. After examining the Bible, the *philosophes* came to the conclusion that its revelations lacked this requirement for truth, since there were patent discrepancies between one passage and another. Both Judaic and

[3] Denis Diderot, *Conversation with the Abbé Barthélemy.* Quoted from *Diderot, Interpreter of Nature: Selected Writings,* tr. by Jean Stewart and Jonathan Kemp (London, 1937), pp. 199–200.

Christian commentators for centuries had made efforts to conciliate the flagrant contradictions, but when eighteenth-century German Biblical scholars and laymen like Voltaire tackled the same texts they concluded that the conciliations were artificial and preposterous. The spirit of logical mathematical consistency which cannot endure contradiction was a potent weapon in the hands of lay intellectuals who judged the documents of the church by this standard.

Even more destructive of accepted religious doctrine was the inductive method which the French *philosophes* acknowledged they learned from the Elizabethan Francis Bacon. As a matter of fact, laboratory scientists were not much influenced by Bacon's exposition of the experimental method of science. His eighteenth-century fame was due primarily to the accident that his method of drawing generalizations a posteriori, after a set of natural experiments had been completed, impressed the *philosophes* as a sure means of arriving at truth. The Baconian emphasis on the facts of experience as the source of scientific law became a methodological bludgeon in the hands of the intellectuals, who condemned as superstitions all sorts of explanations about the physical universe sanctified only in patristic and scholastic literature. The Baconian emphasis on the experimental method led the *philosophes* to discredit anything which was not in conformity with normal everyday experience and which could not be examined for truth or falsehood by experience. For them the only kind of reality was objective and scientific, the only phenomena allowable those which could be apprehended by the senses. Miracles failed to meet the crucial test. They were strange effects which could not be accounted for by direct natural causes. The religious explanation of their origin was not in conformity with the facts of experience and the workings of natural law in a world which was rational. Diderot argued:

You see, once one sets foot in this realm of the supernatural, there are no bounds, one doesn't know where one is going nor what one may meet. Someone affirms that five thousand persons have been fed with five small loaves; this is fine! But to-morrow another will assure you that he fed five thousand people with one small loaf, and the following day a third will have fed five thousand with the wind.[4]

At a time when the churches of Europe recognized the existence of angels and devils the *philosophes* demanded that these beliefs submit themselves to the canons of experience. Since no one could prove their existence from experience, they insisted that they were only figments of the imagination, or fabrications of priests who imposed untruths upon mankind.

There was a third set of propositions which fortified the polemics of the French intellectuals against revealed religion, and this was the doctrine of John Locke set forth in the *Essay Concerning Human Understanding* (1690). Along with Newton and Bacon he is one of the seminal thinkers whose writings the *philosophes* imported from England and disseminated throughout Europe. Locke taught that there was nothing in the intellect which had not previously been in the senses, and that the senses received their impressions directly from nature, from the external world. This thesis, in its simplified form, was as revolutionary a doctrine for the study of man in society as Newton's world-machine had been for a comprehension of the physical universe. The Christian view of the world had posited an immortal soul

4 *Ibid.,* p. 200.

which was given and taken away by God and was the center of conflict between good and evil. This soul of man could grasp divine principles which were absolute truths; it could be moved by divine intervention; unless it were corrupted it recognized the truths of religion and the foundations of authority in the state. But what if there were no soul and man's reason were merely the result of combinations of sensations, as the French philosopher Etienne de Condillac (1715–1780) expounded in the wake of Locke? If all knowledge and the reasoning power itself originated in sensations which were mere reflections of the external world, if they were not God-given, then the absolutes upon which the state and society were presumably based would crumble. Ideas of God, the divine right of kings, immortality, and state authority derived from mere sensory perceptions, nothing more. They were not unalterable. Man-made, they could be modified or abandoned. Though Locke himself never ventured that far, his theory of the source of knowledge led men to question every basic premise of society, to try to find out how many of these ideas, no longer revered as religious absolutes, were actually based on falsehoods inculcated into man and written upon the *tabula rasa*, the clean slate of his mind, after birth.

The Assault on Christianity

The intellectuals leveled their guns upon organized state religions which in the first half of the century were still powerful, vital, even controlling forces in men's lives. Unlike most previous critics of the Christian church, the *philosophes* were no mere heretics or deviators from true doctrine. They struck at the very roots of the church. The theological disputations of the sixteenth and the seventeenth centuries were as nothing compared to this battle to the death between the secular intellectuals and the church. It was their avowed purpose to demolish the citadel.

Among intellectuals of this persuasion Christianity came to be regarded as a pernicious plot which had been hatched in order to turn the earth over to the oppressive powers of a priestly class. The annals of Christianity were to them a chronicle of lies and crimes, and the day it was wiped out, the more sanguine philosophers believed, all the ills of suffering humanity would disappear along with it. Those worldly abuses with which the Christian church had become associated historically were judged to be the essence of the faith. The whole of revealed—as contrasted with natural—religion, in any of its forms, was nothing but an absurd imposition upon the ignorant. A French Catholic historian of thought has called this attack on the church the Trial of God, the God of the Protestants as well as the God of the Catholics.[5] No longer did men debate the fine points of theological doctrine or the forms of religious rites; they now questioned the role of God himself. Men wondered whether they lived in a world governed by a God who was watching over their immortal souls or whether they were merely subject to laws of nature which had at some remote time been set into motion by a Prime Mover whom deists chose to call God. Discussions on the existence of God were passionate in the salons of the nobility and the *bourgeoisie* and in the correspondence of intellectuals and kings.

The weapons of assault of the philosophers on Christianity were learning, wit, scorn, humor, and mockery, the exposure of a tawdry reality beneath the veil of false piety.

[5] This section follows the account by Paul Hazard, *La Pensée Européene au XVIII* *e* *siècle* (Paris, 1946), I, 38–77.

Religion was struck at because it was not rational. Even more, it was attacked as a patent fraud, the artifice of those who controlled the instruments of the cult. Most powerful of the harangues against what Voltaire called the "infamous thing" were those which depicted the thousands upon thousands of victims of intolerance among all the revealed religions of the world. Christianity was judged by simple human standards of good and evil. If its priests were hypocrites who transgressed every tenet of the moral code, if the church in the name of purity of doctrine sanctioned the bloody carnage of fellow Christians, then Christianity, far from being sacred and holy, was a wicked institution which had kept mankind in a terrible thralldom and prevented the attainment of peace, harmony, and progress among the peoples of the earth.

Apologies for Christianity were not lacking, and all sorts of devices were employed to render religion palatable to the age. Pious polemicists identified Christianity with Reason and assumed the premises of their opponents as their point of departure; or they identified God and Nature, winding up in a sentimental pantheism which soon merged with other currents into the mainstream of romanticism. English divines were especially adept in contriving outlandish testimonials to the truth of Christianity, such as the *Trial of the Witnesses of the Resurrection of Jesus* (1729), in which a jury of Englishmen, after hearing the evidence as if they were in a court of law, formally found the apostles not guilty of false witness. As a body of polemical writing the eighteenth-century apologies for Christianity were turgid and verbose, rather trivial, wanting in grandeur of style and thought. No one crossed rapiers with Voltaire.

Through the 1760's Christian religions, enthroned in Eu-

ropean polities as state religions, could still command obedience through the intervention of the secular arm—get a few
hundred anticlerical writers imprisoned, have the public
executioner make a bonfire of their books, force the hanging
of a man who was accused of sacrilege, try people for witch-
craft, and even burn victims in *autos-da-fé*. By the last
decades before the Revolution, the doctrines of the church
were no longer secure enough to permit many such per-
secutions. The philosophers were thoroughly aware that
they had fomented a revolution in the fundamental beliefs
of their fellow men. Voltaire reported on each new triumph
of philosophy against the church with the exultation of a
commander winning battles. When the pope, acceding to
universal demand, dissolved the Jesuit order in 1773, he was
awarding the philosophers the palm of victory with his own
hand and leaving them the field.

Frederick II of Prussia (1712–1786), with characteristic
shrewdness, had already read the signs of the times some
two decades earlier. In his confidential *Political Testament
of 1752* he dismissed the pope as "an old neglected idol in
his niche. . . . His thunderbolts are extinguished. His policy is known. Instead of laying peoples under interdict and
deposing sovereigns as of yore, he is satisfied if no one de-
poses him and lets him say Mass peacefully in St. Peter's." [6]

[6] *Die Politischen Testamente Friedrich's des Grossen*, ed. by
Gustav Berthold Volz (Berlin, 1920), p. 47.

CHAPTER III

The Moral and Political Outlook

THE vast increase in factual knowledge about the physical universe gave men a tremendous sense of power, a feeling that with this newly acquired knowledge they could dominate nature. This new consciousness of power justified abandonment of the vain search for first principles and primary causes. If man could manipulate matter and conform it to his will, what difference did it make what matter was? The mediaeval conception of human impotence gave way to a marvelous surge of self-confidence, a buoyancy, an optimism which, though at times it was diluted by grave misgivings and doubts, remained overwhelmingly the spirit of the age.

While the mediaeval philosophers had been absorbed with beatitude, and Protestantism had brought turmoil into the breasts of true believers over whether or not they had grace and would be saved, the eighteenth-century man of letters set the problem of terrestrial happiness at the dead center of morals. The primary question was whether man could be happy on earth. Christian moralists had taught that man was born to toil, to suffer, and to lament, for he carried the weight of the Biblical curse and of Adam's original sin. As a response to the same problem, dominant eighteenth-century opinion was convinced that man was capable of great happiness now and in this world, irrespective of any future drama which might be enacted in heaven or hell. Concentration upon the "pursuit of happiness" in this world is magnificently expressed in the language of the American Declaration of Independence, composed by revolutionaries who had been profoundly influenced by the *philosophes*.

Most thinkers inclined to the idea that man was born with a capacity for happiness: witness the idealization in the travel literature of the age of the life of primitive savages in a state of nature, especially the fortunate inhabitants of recently discovered Tahiti. To rebut those who believed in the Christian doctrine of the essential sinfulness of man, the travel-book writers—those who had ventured to the new worlds as well as those who had written about the blessed isles in their Paris garrets—depicted the simplicity, beauty, and happiness of primitive man. What need had he of the terrible Christian epic of the fall and man's sin and redemption? The noble savage seemed to hail from another planet untouched by sermons depicting the tortures of hell and the sufferings of a Man-God, and he was happier and more virtuous for his ignorance. In the exotic literature there was thus gathered a profusion of "scientific evidence"—as the intellectuals understood it—on one of the overriding problems of man, his capacity for contentment on earth.

When thinkers of the day asked themselves how natural man had lost his original state of happiness, their anticlericalism guided them to an easy answer: they pointed an accusing finger at the priests of all nations. Revealed religions had taught that the human body and its enjoyment were evil, had imposed upon man laws of moral conduct which were directly contrary to his nature, and thus had brought him endless grief. Christianity was the target for the most vitriolic attacks because of its denial of the pleasures of the flesh; by contrast, Mohammedanism, which had been more tolerant of man's natural desires, usually fared better in the imaginative writings of the intellectuals.

Liberation of the Passions

Absorption in terrestrial happiness had as a concomitant a general emancipation of the emotions and the passions, which no longer had to be held forever in check as the real sources of wrongdoing. Passions were the very savor of life, which would be rendered insipid without them. They were the winds which set the sails in motion, and though on occasion they might drive the boat on the rocks, they were essential parts of the natural order. This eulogy of the free expression of emotion led to an idealization of sexual love in a form which later came to be known as romanticism. The attainment of romantic love replaced the attainment of heavenly bliss, and depiction of the sufferings and trials of the hero and the heroine in the working out of their affairs replaced the drama of Christ as the story of mankind. Eighteenth-century novels and tales usually ended with fulfillment, a long series of reaffirmations that man could achieve happiness on earth.

The tear ducts of mankind were opened and men were allowed to give vent to their sensibility in a lachrymose manner without suffering the accusation that they were effeminate. Great men became proud rather than ashamed of their emotions and one of the most extravagant and influential figures of the modern world, Jean-Jacques Rousseau, wrote a voluminous book of *Confessions* which is the history of his feelings and sentiments, each one of which he relished

again in the retelling. The book invites contrast with the
Confessions of St. Augustine, for whom life's struggle was
a search for God. In this age of sensibility all emotions were
good and a virtuous man unloosed them freely. Tears of
joy and tears of grief were intermingled. Readers wept profusely with Rousseau's *Julie* and shared with Goethe *The
Sorrows of Young Werther.*

Pleasure was recognized by the *philosophes* to be a legiti-
mate good and was freed from the mediaeval Christian and
Calvinist anathemas. Pleasure was conceived as a spontaneous
human response to good and evil. Since in its sexual form
it was associated with the reproduction of the species, what
better proof that pleasure was necessary and useful and not
a manifestation of man's lower nature as most Christian
doctrines had held? In the past, the life of reason, the way
of the philosopher, Greek, Hebrew, or Christian, had generally required emancipation from the desires of the flesh.
The eighteenth century saw no incompatibility between the
philosopher's world and sensual pleasure. "I am a very volup-
tuous philosopher," said Voltaire.

Moral Philosophy: The Laws of Nature

Idealization of the state of nature took on characteristics
of a cult, retaining the angels and devils of Christianity in a
different guise. Before man was misled from the path of
nature, he had absolute liberty and life was blissful. But alas!
humanity had been perverted by the impositions of despots
and priests, who were the Lucifer and cohorts of the natural
order. These wicked ones introduced strange objects and
manners into nature which warped its perfection. Whenever man falls or is pushed from nature, whenever he vio-
lates the true laws of universal conduct by following petty

conventionalities, he suffers the worldly punishment of the new deity—he is unhappy. Thus all the ills of existing society and the wretchedness of man are to be understood as the inevitable result of deviation from the prescribed laws of man's instinctive being. The eighteenth-century *philosophe* entreated man to forsake his artificial ways, to live according to the laws of the *Système de la nature*, and thus to recapture the happiness from which Christian civilization had long barred him.

For the intellectuals were firmly convinced that there were laws governing man's actions in society—laws which could be discovered in precisely the same manner that natural scientists had reached their conclusions. These rules of conduct which embodied the laws of society were generally defined as morals or moral philosophy. "I believed," wrote the French philosopher Claude Helvétius (1715–1771), "that morals should be treated like all other sciences, and that one should arrive at a moral principle as one proceeds with an experiment in physics." [1] The moral laws thus scientifically derived would be useful to society. Just as physical laws of science had led to technological inventions and progress in mechanical arts, so the formulation of moral laws would result in greater social progress for humanity. Once the immutable laws of society were made known men would inevitably follow them, human institutions would be molded in accordance with their dictates, and greater happiness for all mankind would ensue.

The method of arriving at laws of social or moral science having been declared identical with that of physical science, the intellectuals proceeded to their laboratories. Most of them were so impressed by the great conquests of the

[1] Claude Helvétius, *De l'esprit*, in *Oeuvres* (London, 1776), I, ii.

physicists, who with a few crucial experiments had revolutionized the whole view of the universe, that they entertained similar expectations for the science of man and society. History and contemporary travel literature were the only laboratories of experience in morals open to the intellectuals. They were reluctant to examine objectively the European man of their own times with whom they were most familiar; since he appeared to them caked over with a crust of false conventions, they deduced that little could be learned about true moral man from observing him.

Unfortunately, the men of letters who manipulated historical examples as scientific proof positive of their theories of society were absurdly superficial and casual in assembling their data. They contented themselves with a few illustrations pulled at random from classical literature or from authors who had compiled books about the customs of the Chinese or the Indians. Thus in their voluminous writings on man in society philosophers of every tendency came to use historical data in much the same manner that a preacher quotes a text from Scripture before he proceeds with his sermon. The eighteenth-century theorists have left us great insights on the nature of social relations, but these were really intuitions, not propositions derived in accordance with the scientific method to which they gave lip service.

As defined by the intellectuals, the moral laws were universal and changeless. They were simple and easy of comprehension, not hieratic, not the secret of priests and learned doctors. They were commonly perceived, not dependent upon sudden illumination or grace. The Declaration of Independence held certain truths to be self-evident, immediately knowable, without the necessity of elucidation by schoolmen. The ready communicability of the moral laws was an attribute especially convenient to the intellectual reformers, who with high purpose undertook to make them known to great numbers of people. In a word, they became popular propagandists for the truths of moral philosophy. The British essayist Joseph Addison (1672–1719) wrote in an early number of his periodical *The Spectator:* "It was said of Socrates, that he brought philosophy down from heaven, to inhabit among men: and I shall be ambitious to have it said of me, that I have brought philosophy out of closets and libraries, schools and colleges, to dwell in clubs and assemblies, at tea-tables and in coffee-houses." [2] The moral laws would be pabulum for the men in the street—and for the ladies too. Everybody could become a philosopher by learning the moral laws.

Self-Love and Benevolence

The doctrine of self-love, an axiom in their whole science of society, raised a primary ethical problem for the moral philosophers. Since they believed that man was born good and was also born with self-love, they had to find this passion a source of ultimate good rather than evil. But how conciliate the separate self-loves of individuals in a social state? On this point the French intellectuals differed from some of their British counterparts. The French tried to prove that if all men acted in accordance with their self-love a harmony of these self-loves would somehow prevail in the order of society and men would be happy. They pointed to society's existing confusion and dogmatically affirmed that it had been created by the artificial barriers set up by states and religions to the free expression of this self-love. Inflexibly ra-

[2] *The Spectator in Eight Volumes* (Edinburgh, n.d.), no. 10, March 12, 1711, I, 43.

tionalist, the French would recognize no other drive for action except self-love. Voltaire, as always, gave it the classic epigrammatic definition:

Those who have said that love of ourselves is the basis of all our opinions and all our actions, have therefore been quite right in India, Spain, and all the habitable world: and as one does not write to prove to men that they have faces, it is not necessary to prove to them that they have self-love. Self-love is our instrument of preservation; it resembles the instrument which perpetuates the species. It is necessary, it is dear to us, it gives us pleasure, and it has to be hidden.[3]

The British school of moralists avoided the rather mechanical view of the Frenchmen by positing the existence of certain natural moral sentiments of sympathy which served to bind individual men together. Benevolence, a feeling of sympathy toward one's fellow man, was a passion as strong as self-love and in an ideal state of society would serve to regulate the social harmony. To the British thinkers humanitarian sympathy was a cohesive element in society; in the next century it came to be the basis of utilitarianism. As against the wolvine bestiality of man depicted by Thomas Hobbes in the previous age, the eighteenth-century sentimentalist, without doing violence to his trust in reason, believed that pity, compassion, fellow feeling—in short, benevolence—were woven into the very constitution of man. Man was a social creature who naturally loved the fellow of his species, was moved by the suffering or happiness of others, and had a tendency to do good to his neighbors. The British clergyman and novelist Laurence Sterne (1713–1768) wrote an impassioned hymn to man's

[3] *Voltaire's Philosophical Dictionary*, p. 272.

natural sensibility and benevolence. "I feel some joys and generous cares beyond myself—all comes from thee, great —great Sensorium of the world! which vibrates, if a hair of our heads but falls upon the ground, in the remotest desert of thy creation." [4]

The Science of Economics

A doctrine of enlightened self-interest or self-love served as the basic preconception of the new science of economics, which was really born in this age. From the beginning, two trends of thought emerged: the theories of the French physiocrats, who tended to emphasize the importance of land in the nation's economy, and the principles of Adam Smith (1723–1790), who revealed the wealth which lay in a nation's industrial and commercial enterprise. Whatever the technical differences in their points of view, however, they stood together in denouncing the regulatory system of economy which had survived from the Middle Ages in a wilderness of local prohibitions against free enterprise—the natural expression of self-interest—and in attacking the restrictive state decrees which had been set up by seventeenth-century bullionists and mercantilists. If individual economic man were only allowed free play in society, the competing individual interests, without state intervention, would form a pattern which would produce the most real wealth and hence happiness among the nations of the world. The treatise by Adam Smith is not designed to show one state how to beat the other in a struggle for commercial supremacy. It is called *Enquiry into the Nature and Causes of the Wealth of Nations* (1776), with emphasis on the plural,

[4] Lawrence Sterne, *A Sentimental Journey through France and Italy* (1768). Quoted from the 1926 edition (New York), p. 161.

and is a book of economic laws to be followed by all men. In a world where whole new continents invited exploitation, there was enough for everybody.

The Politics of the Philosophes

On the whole the *philosophes* were concerned with the basic moral preconceptions and attributes of their society, and not with the precise form of its political institutions. They wanted to emancipate society from what they considered the superstitions and restraints of the past, and to provide it with a rational machinery. But once society was free and governed in accordance with the laws of reason, the philosophers rested on the comfortable assumption that progress, justice, and the good life were assured. Monarchy, aristocracy, or republic—the question did not appear to be of paramount importance. The principles of reason could be clothed in any vestments. There was perhaps a tendency to prefer monarchical stability in a regime with liberal guarantees above other traditional government forms described by the political theorists, but in general the issue had no burning partisans.

> For forms of government let fools contest;
> Whate'er is best administer'd is best.

rhymed Alexander Pope (1688–1744) in his *Essay on Man.*[5]

The *philosophes* were gradualists. In their scheme of things, the emancipation of society was to take place without the abruptness and blind brutal force of revolution. In the past, change had been cataclysmic because mankind

[5] Alexander Pope, *Essay on Man* (1733). Quoted from *The Works of the English Poets*, ed. by Samuel Johnson (London, 1810), XII, 225.

moved in ignorance of the law of its own development. Fury and violence were the consequence of failure to perceive that gradual progress was inevitable. Now that men knew the law of human crises, the same progress which once engendered disorder could be achieved by a slow and peaceful transformation. This emphatic disavowal of revolutionary action was no mere subterfuge to avoid the prosecutions of the state. It was a cardinal principle entirely congruent with their universal philosophy. Even those who foretold the boldest of social innovations, such as basic alterations in the nature of property, posited only smooth transitions.

The intellectuals wanted to perfect, not to uproot and overturn the society in which they lived. They conjured up visions of the perfect state, but they felt no obligation to prescribe a course of political action for achieving it, save by following the laws of nature and reason. They attacked the philosophic foundations of their society, but they rarely sought to undermine its specific institutions. Hence the half-tolerant attitude of kings toward the intellectual *enfants terribles*. The autocrats who invited them to their palaces were not perturbed by the shining utopias of the *philosophes* and even found them amusing. While they would have prosecuted as dangerous to the state any pointed attack on the farming of the salt tax, they could with great show of largesse permit their philosophical coteries to flaunt doctrines about natural rights, atheism, democracy, and even communism.

But men are often unaware of the consequences of their own ideas. Though the intellectuals as a group were opposed to the overthrow of state power by physical violence, they had a tremendous effect in preparing the climate of opin-

ion for the Revolution of 1789. The *philosophes* had so
assiduously undermined the spiritual props of the *ancien
régime* that the very rulers of society ceased to hold fast
to the religion and the system of ideas which had sustained
them. Men have judged the *philosophes* more or less sym-
pathetically depending upon whether the ideals of society
which they helped to demolish have been esteemed or
despised.

Common Ground of the Intellectuals

Despite their sharp cleavages and varying interests, there
was a common ground on which all the intellectuals could
stand, and from their inconsistent and even incompatible
tendencies there emerged a moral outlook distinct from that
of the previous age. The eighteenth-century philosophers
popularized general precepts of conduct which in time were
widely accepted in most civilized societies. They made aggressive war look odious and mocked the ideal of military
glory. They preached religious toleration, free speech, a
free press. They were in favor of the sanctions of law to protect individual liberties and they were against tyranny which
governed by caprice. They wanted equality of all citizens
before the law and they were opposed to any recognition
of social distinctions when men were brought to justice.
They abhorred torture and other barbaric punishments and
pleaded for their abolition; they believed that punishment
should fit the crime and should be imposed only to restrain
potential malefactors. They wanted freedom of movement
across state boundaries both for individuals and articles of
commerce. Most of them believed that it did not require the
threat of eternal torment in hell to make moral ideas generally accepted among mankind. They were convinced that

the overwhelming number of men, if their natural goodness were not perverted in childhood, would act in harmony with simple rules and the dictates of rational principles without the necessity for severe restraints and awful punishments.

In summary, though the *philosophes* did not solve the problem of the existence of evil and suffering in the world, they did manage to establish in European society a general consensus about conduct which is evil, a moral attitude which still sustains us. Despite their subservient behavior toward some of the European despots and the social anarchy ultimately inherent in their doctrines of absolute self-interest, the eighteenth-century men of letters did formulate a set of moral principles which to this day remain basic to any discussion of human rights. The deficiencies of their optimistic moral and political outlook are by now visible, but they did venture the first bold examination of reality since the Greeks and they dared to set forth brand-new abstractions about man and the universe. They taught their contemporaries to view the institutions of church and state in the light of reason and to judge them by the simple criterion of human happiness.

The "Minuet" of Philosophes and Enlightened Despots

There is, of course, a ridiculous aspect to the "minuet" of the philosophers and the enlightened despots. The absolute monarchs in fact did not create the liberal state of the philosophers. At best they introduced the regulated state, at worst the regimented state. The *philosophes* rationalized the power drives of the enlightened despots with the bland assurance that "to be very good you had to be very strong."

There were nevertheless significant points of valid contact between the philosophers and the despots. The monarchs sensed that the philosophers' praise of the Newtonian order of nature and the rationalist spirit was not alien to the basic centralizing policies of their governments. In turn, when they established uniform administrative procedures, they were at least approaching the *philosophes'* ideal of equality before the law. The government of law in accordance with reason and the natural order tended to abolish odious distinctions among men, especially those which annoyed the intellectuals most, the differences between noble and nonnoble. By the eve of the French Revolution, royal power had so effectively curtailed ecclesiastical influence that in reality all the churches of Europe had been transformed into state institutions. Religious toleration in large measure had been granted. The enlightened despots at least in part repaid the *philosophes* for their ideological support.

The six chapters which follow are limited for the most part to the internal political and social conflicts and the international relations of the five major European powers. This does not mean that developments in Scandinavia, the Iberian Peninsula, the Italian and German principalities, and the Balkans lack intrinsic interest. But it is felt that the motive forces at play in the Age of Reason can be illustrated sufficiently well for a book of this compass by drawing upon events in France, Britain, Austria, Prussia, and Russia.

CHAPTER IV

The Realm of France

LOUIS XIV's death in 1715 was hailed by the people of Paris and the courtiers of Versailles with ferocious joy and wild drunkenness. The King's last testament was irreverently broken. Men of high and low degree insulted the cadaver of the Sun King, symbolically foretelling the destruction of the absolute Catholic monarchy of France. For the parsimony and piety imposed on the court in Louis XIV's old age, the Regent and the two Louis's who succeeded him substituted luxurious expenditure and license. In place of an orderly, centralized, and systematic monarchy operated by technicians, many of whom were commoners, the successors of Louis XIV permitted the restoration of real power to the ancient nobility who had been corralled into the palace of Versailles and threw the doors wide open to government by petty intrigue. Advancement, no longer open to talent, was often dictated by what French euphemism calls "gallantry." It has been said that women set the tone of monarchial government in eighteenth-century France. The forty-nine-year reign of the debauched and bored Louis XV is the central fact of political life during this period. The simplicity of his well-meaning and pathetic successor could not affect the character or alter the trend of the regime. In his tragic death on the scaffold in 1793, Louis XVI expiated the sins of the fathers.

The French monarch continued to proclaim himself a king by divine right and an absolute sovereign who was sole fountainhead of law. In a famous speech of 1766 Louis XV declared that he held his power from God and that authority was vested in himself alone, "without sharing or dependence." Viewed historically, these pretensions were by this time absurd: the monarchy was already being tossed about by the currents of opposing classes, and the king's claim to rule by divine right was so irrelevant as to be fatuous. The royal will was no longer transmitted swiftly and efficiently to local officials. The animating force in the state was lacking, since the French king had no initiative or interest in governance.

Ministers, Intendants, and Parlements

Too indifferent and dissolute to rule himself, Louis XV nevertheless refused to allow his ministers to rule for him. He mistrusted his chief advisers, and after Cardinal Fleury's death in 1743 he appointed no other prime minister. The King felt hemmed in by the elaborate bureaucratic mechanism inherited from his predecessor, and seriously impaired its effectiveness through a bewildering turnover of key officials: eighteen foreign secretaries and fourteen controllers-general followed one another in rapid succession. Partly for amusement, partly to circumvent his ministers, the King despatched special agents and emissaries throughout Europe, to work behind their backs and report directly to him. Since there was no prime minister, each major department of state virtually led a life of its own; the controller-general, who was the treasurer, could not co-ordinate or dominate them even though he approached closest to the chief role. This lack of an effective executive either in king or cabinet resulted in a changeling policy dependent upon chance, as the monarchy was buffeted by turbulent economic and social forces in the realm.

The provinces were administered by a group of noble officials known as Intendants of Justice, Police, and Finances. In name they were the subordinate representatives of the controller-general, endowed with broad powers of taxation, general administration, and justice, and many subsidiary functions relative to the policing of commerce and industry. But these men were proud officials of independent means, not obsequious civil servants in any modern sense of the term. The Intendants conceived of themselves as protectors of the local interests in their provinces and often in practice they mitigated the severity of laws emanating from Paris. It is significant of the new administrative relationships under the French monarchy of the eighteenth century that the Intendants were no longer the battering rams of a royal absolutism as they had been under Richelieu and Louis XIV.

The greatest counterpoise to the monarchy were the provincial judicial bodies, the *parlements*—foremost in prestige among them the *Parlement* of Paris—whose duty it was to adjudicate disputes at law and to register royal decrees. By refusing to act on such decrees, the *parlements* could often force upon the king amendments and modifications which they favored. The line of demarcation between the administrative functions of public law and the judicial functions of private law was shadowy. The king's ministers flagrantly interfered in what were clearly issues of private suits and the *parlements* sought to influence the public administration of the kingdom. The *Parlement* of Paris, above all others, tried to assume powers similar to those of the contemporary English Parliament, or to usurp prerogatives of the old French Estates-General which had not met since 1614.

There was a bitter struggle between the monarchy and the *parlements* throughout the reigns of Louis XV and Louis XVI. *Parlements* tore down posted royal orders on the pretext that they had not been properly registered, and the kings of France "exiled" refractory *parlements*. This conflict at no time had the character of a war between defenders of democratic liberty and upholders of royal absolutism. On the contrary, the *parlement* was always the juridical voice of the aristocracy. A well-organized offensive was spearheaded by the nobility of the robe, who controlled the *parlements* and aimed to revive traditional aristocratic powers long suppressed by the kings of France. As the guardian of special privilege embodied in custom, the *parlement* set itself in stubborn opposition to the royal administrators who were laboring to establish laws and practices applicable to all subjects of the monarch irrespective of their social status. Despite the King's unconcern, his administrators in the very performance of their office tended to rationalize the government of France, to eliminate the confusing residues of the feudal system, the restrictions on free commerce within the realm, the multifarious taxing systems which weighed unequally on different classes and areas, and the wholesale exemption of persons and estates from bearing a just share in the burdens of government. In *parlement* the feudal spirit, fortified with legal precedents, lived on into the eighteenth century.

The King could issue *lettres de cachet*, sealed orders which sent men to the Bastille without recourse to any French equivalent of habeas corpus or the English trial by jury. At the behest of a mistress he might irresponsibly dismiss one of his chief ministers. Since Louis XV governed by caprice when he governed at all, he had neither the will nor the power to impose a royal absolutism on France, and in the day-to-day conduct of affairs he was not the generator of energy for the organization of the state. Administrative offices and army ranks were bought and sold. Posts were acquired by inheritance. There was an army of bureaucrats who could not be dispossessed without upsetting the whole governmental system, since men who held office had a proprietary right which was protected by law. Far from carrying through administrative reorganizations as other continental monarchs were doing, Louis XV relaxed the decrees put into effect by his great-grandfather and made substantial concessions to local privilege. In some respects his reign signalized a retrogression to the diversity and confusion of earlier centuries, leaving France an administrative patchwork unequal to the economic and military problems which confronted this, the greatest state in Europe.

At the close of the Seven Years' War in 1763 the national debt had mounted to over 1,700,000,000 *livres* (the *livre* was the basic monetary unit before the introduction of the *franc* in 1795); it was further augmented by the costs of participation in the War for American Independence. Interest alone on the national debt jumped from 18,000,000 *livres* in the middle of the century to 106,000,000 by 1776. The actual debt was not staggering, except in terms of the anomalies of the French political system. The state was whirling in a vicious fiscal circle: no further loans could be secured unless the King levied extraordinary taxes as a guarantee that money would be available to repay the creditors. But the tax burden could not be spread without attacking the exemptions of the clergy and the nobility. The idea of state bankruptcy, though suggested, was an abhorrent breach of faith which Louis XVI could not entertain. To end the impasse an Estates-General was called and a chain reaction of revolutionary events was set in motion which destroyed the monarchy—and along with it the nobility and the clergy.

The Nobles

Although in theory the unwritten ancient constitution of the kingdom divided the subjects of the French king into three estates—the clergy, the nobility, and a catch-all known as the third estate—in practice there was only one underlying criterion of differentiation, the distinction between a man who was noble and a man who was not. The same division existed among the clergy as among the laity, for great ecclesiastical offices were sinecures restricted to aristocratic families, and the humble parish priest was always a commoner.

There were various gradations of dignity among the nobles themselves. Enjoying the highest social status were those families who held titles by "race," by inheritance, and who were therefore considered truly noble; of these many had offices or sinecures in the army. Traditionally, such a hereditary noble was one who could trace his aristocratic progenitors back to "time immemorial," but by the end of the seventeenth century, four generations was usually considered ample fulfillment of the requirement. The nobles of race and the nobles of the sword looked with disdain upon all other nobles—those whose title had been secured by royal

letter, whose escutcheon merely came along with the purchase of an honorific office or a great fief, or who had been
rewarded for municipal service or a substantial loan to the
royal treasury. It was Louis XIV who had broken the power
of the old nobility by frequent recourse to the act of selling
ennoblement by letter patent. In order to get more money
into the royal treasury, such noble titles from time to time
were revoked and renewed, a practice which did not add
to the prestige of the estate.

Contemporary estimates of the total number of persons
who held authentic titles of nobility of any sort diverged
widely, from 80,000 to five times that figure. By the end of
the century, the crucial mark of distinction among the horde
of ancient and upstart nobles was the test of presentability
at court. In 1789 there were about 20,000 whom it was
proper to receive at Versailles, supposedly in conformity
with a decree which limited the privilege to hereditary nobles who could trace their ancestry back to the year 1400.
If the edict had ever been enforced literally, the palace
would have been desolate.

By the eighteenth century certain administrative and judicial offices were restricted to men bearing noble titles:
the intendancies, the magistracies in the *Parlement* of Paris,
the secretaryships in the Chamber of Accounts; also the
higher ecclesiastical posts of archbishop and of abbot, and
the chief military ranks. As titles of nobility grew common,
there was a tendency for members of the great official bodies, in defense of their prestige, to impose ever more stringent
entrance requirements of nobility upon prospective incum-
bents. In general, nobles of the sword controlled the army
and nobles of the robe conducted the administration of the
kingdom. Of this latter group a few families had secured

by tradition a virtual monopoly of the great intendancies and of the presidencies of the *parlements*.

The nobles were divided among themselves not only in terms of symbols of dignity and office, but in economic power. The nobility of the sword, which was bedizened with the grandest titles, was often the poorer element, dependent almost exclusively on royal bounty. Among the nobility of the robe, the judicial and administrative officers who had the more recent titles, there were men of wealth who retained relationships with the great *bourgeois* and were sometimes not to be distinguished from them. The way of life of the country nobility, at the bottom of the scale of aristocracy, was not wholly unlike that of the more prosperous peasants.

Apart from their monopoly of various offices, nobles enjoyed a host of special privileges which made the title sought after for more than the honor it conferred. They were free from many taxes normally levied on commoners; they had the right to be tried in a court of their peers; they were exempt from humiliating punishments. In law these privileges could be abrogated if a noble demeaned himself with degrading occupations such as trade and manufacture, or if he committed vile deeds, but the procedure was not resorted to frequently.

A noble could fight, judge, or rule; it was a "disparagement" if he participated directly in increasing the wealth of France. Since the administration was not expanding, and the army could not absorb an ever-increasing number of officers, toward the end of the old regime there were not nearly enough functions appropriate to noble status to go round. Prevented by the mores of their caste from engaging in commerce or industry, and often trained for nothing but elegant display, large numbers of aristocrats were condemned to parasitic idleness.

There was nothing hidden or startling about the decomposition of France's court nobility in the closing decades of the eighteenth century. The symptoms of its decay had long been written on its face. The nobles of France gained for themselves the invidious hatred of their nearest rivals by snubbing commoners who were rich and talented. The aristocrats suffered general public contempt because of their scandalous lives and the corruption of their morals in defiance of all precepts of the Catholic religion. During a trial before the *Parlement* of Paris (the famous case of the diamond necklace), a cardinal of the church, a Rohan, scion of the ancient hereditary nobility of France, stood accused in general opinion of attempting adultery upon the person of the Queen herself.

Eighteenth-century France had become a strange, chaotic combination, hardly an amalgam, of the strong centralizing monarchical absolutism created by Louis XIV and the spirit of noble independence resurgent after his death. The memory of the *Fronde* was not dead in France, and there were repeated attempts on the part of the nobility to recoup powers of which they had been divested in the previous century. Paradoxical as it may now seem, the first call for the Estates-General in 1787 setting the stage for the Revolution was a consequence of aristocratic pressure on the weakened bankrupt monarchy. The nobility dreamed of an aristocratic reaction, a reversion to a mediaeval constitutional ideal in which their role was predominant in council. Instead they unleashed the new social and economic classes of the third estate.

The Peasants

There were more than 20,000,000 peasants in France who, though still subject to a host of manorial dues—payments in money, labor, or kind which they owed their lords—in the overwhelming majority were free men who tilled their own lands. The French peasant was by no means among the most wretched in Europe, since he was emancipated from most of the disabilities of serfdom. He was not bound to the soil he worked, and he could raise his children in such occupations as he liked; moreover, he was frequently protected by law and custom from arbitrary dispossession of his farm by the local lord. He was probably more prosperous than the peasants of other lands on the continent, and he certainly enjoyed a greater measure of freedom. But travelers compared him with the English farmer, and were struck by the contrast in vitality and well-being. One contemporary observer wrote:

The portion of the taxes which he pays according to his rate of industry, is either so unjustly estimated, so exorbitant, or levied in so discouraging a manner, that a farmer is afraid of clearing a new field, of augmenting the number of his cattle, or in short of displaying fresh industry, sure as he is to see himself loaded with a new arbitrary tax, though he has not sufficient to pay the old one. . . . It is a maxim received in France, that the Peasantry must be kept low, and not suffered to be at ease. But supposing this maxim to be as true as it is destitute of humanity, at least, nothing is more certain than that it has been abused. So far from being at their ease, the peasants in France have not even a necessary subsistence. They are a species of men, which begins to decline and wear out at the age of forty, for want of a reparation . . . proportioned to its fatigues. Humanity is hurt by the comparison of them with other men, and above all with the

English peasants. Observe but the French labourers, and their exterior alone points out the impairs of their bodies, and the destruction of the faculties of their minds.[1]

In a country overwhelmingly agricultural, the unwholesomeness of economic policies which discouraged production and depressed the peasantry was obvious.

During the century there were fifteen or twenty crop failures and the small peasants were threatened by periodic famine. Their discontent reached a climax during the general economic crisis which swept France during the last three years of the ancient regime. The peasants, always hungry for more land, saw with resentment vast uncultivated areas belonging to a local lord or to a religious establishment. Many nobles had ceased to perform any useful functions on their estates; they were absentee owners who spent most of the year in town, delegating authority to a steward whose person and power were not sanctified by tradition. Since the nobility no longer rendered any services, they were finally forfeiting the respect considered due to righteous lords. In 1789 the peasants of France were not in the vanguard of the revolution against the state, but once the bars of authority were let down they were quick to sack the châteaux which housed the records of their manorial dues and to seize whatever land they could.

The Industrial Workers

The only substantial large-scale manufacturing was concentrated in the cloth centers of the northern and the south-

[1] [Plumard de Dangeul], *Remarks on the Advantages of France and of Great Britain with Respect to Commerce and to the Other Means of Encreasing the Wealth and Power of a State*, tr. from the French original (London, 1754), pp. 16–17.

ern provinces. While mediaeval guild regulations prohibiting the free movement of artisans from place to place and the free hiring of workers for manufactures nominally remained in force, the code was often violated without the imposition of legal sanctions. At times, whole manufacturing areas and specific new industries were granted a blanket exemption from guild restrictions by royal decree.

Most workers were not exclusively engaged in industry but alternated factory work with agriculture, even where the putting-out system had been abandoned for a central factory in a town. Therefore numerical estimates of the number of industrial workers in France in the last century of the old regime have a wide spread. Inspector of Manufactures Roland wrote in his article in Diderot's *Encyclopédie* that a figure of 150,000 would cover men, women, and children in industry, but other contemporary figures are far higher. In any case, the total could hardly have exceeded 1 or 2 per cent of the population. The bulk of ordinary manufacturing was still conducted in tiny units of masters, journeymen, and apprentices under the old guild system.

During the reign of Louis XIV, Colbert had sent spies abroad to bring back new industrial techniques, had sponsored the experiments of inventors in special laboratories, had enticed foreign entrepreneurs with concessions, and had attracted skilled workers with special privileges. In the eighteenth century, although the government manifested much less enthusiasm in pursuit of this policy, it was not completely abandoned. As England was undergoing its industrial revolution, a few models of the new water- or steam-driven textile machines, particularly those used in spinning, were smuggled out of the country in spite of prohibitions and embargoes. And in the last years of the old regime an ambitious group of manufacturers in Rouen, the Abbé Baudeau's Free Society for the Encouragement of Inventions Which Tend to Perfect Arts and Trades, in Imitation of the London Society (1776), and government agencies working under the minister Calonne made a concerted effort to further the introduction of machines and new industrial processes in mining and manufacturing. The workers received the machines with complaints that they deprived them of jobs, disrupted the organization of the existing industrial system, and caused a marked deterioration in the quality of the finished product. But since the use of the new mechanical devices was limited, and power for the most part was still manually supplied, machine-breaking by enraged artisans was not a serious problem. Except for chance outbreaks which were easily silenced, there was no co-ordinated movement of violence against the introduction of machinery.

In the course of the century the price of bread—and this single item of consumption normally absorbed well over 50 per cent of the average laborer's total expenditures— remained fairly stable, possibly showing a slight increase. Wages rose somewhat, though in most occupations they were fixed at traditional levels. When they moved upward rather spottily in the last decades before the Revolution they still usually lagged behind prices. Strikes for higher wages were rather more disciplined than the outbursts of workers in the preceding age, and journeymen in a number of skilled trades, who formed secret organizations, on occasion wielded the strike weapon with remarkable success. At other times the royal police intervened and, as in previous centuries, unceremoniously hanged the strike leaders in the public square.

The factory workers, hard hit by the depression of 1787, joined in the Revolution of 1789. On the Great Days when peasants sacked châteaux they wrecked new machinery, but as a class the small industrial proletariat were no more important protagonists of the Revolution than the peasants.

The Bourgeois

In provincial cities which were trading centers, the great *bourgeois* were hardly differentiated in their manner of living from the nobility. The division of the city of Rennes into three residential areas about the middle of the century is more typical of the realities of class stratification than nominal distinctions by estate: there was an area of grand houses for nobles and rich *bourgeois;* a section in the old city inhabited by artisans and shopkeepers; and a suburban area where common laborers lived. In provincial capitals such as Dijon, about a third of the inhabitants belonged to the families of functionaries who, whether or not they had a noble title of recent origin, tended to be *bourgeois* in spirit. The top financiers and tax farmers who were creditors of the state and of many of the hereditary noble families aped the grandeur of princes of the blood and were not noted for the practice of those virtues of sobriety and parsimony traditionally associated with the French *bourgeois*. Standing nearest to the great nobility, the rich *bourgeois* imitated their ostentation and extravagance. Unable to achieve equality in status with the hereditary nobility, the financiers tried to approach them through equality in vice; this was the censorious historical judgment of the nineteenth-century French moralist, Alexis de Tocqueville.

But if there was a superficial measure of similarity in

manners, the difference in the changing economic position of the two classes was real and in the end decisive. The eighteenth century saw the burgeoning of a prosperous merchant class in France, while the ancient nobility, unlike its English counterpart across the Channel, refused to join in the direction of profitable enterprise, considering it a degradation. The foreign commerce of France quintupled between 1716 and 1789, and as the commercial profits accumulated from the sale of wine, brandy, West Indian sugar, textiles, and luxury goods, they were invested in new industrial projects—coal and iron mines, glass works, metal plants and textile factories—which brought increasing wealth to the *bourgeois* entrepreneurs. The enrichment of the merchant and manufacturer is not paralleled by any equivalent rise in the prosperity of other classes in the realm. Some nobles invested in commerce and industry and reaped their share of the profits even when they did not actually manage the ventures, but they were clearly the exception. Most successful were the merchants of port cities such as Marseilles, Bordeaux, Nantes, Rouen, who traded with the American colonies, the Orient, and other parts of Europe, processing and exchanging the products of all of them, as well as exporting native French goods. Their vast new wealth was soon reflected in the good fortune of the professional men who served them and lived in their company—the doctors, the lawyers, and the intellectuals. Ownership of land remained the mark of gentility, and to acquire it the great *bourgeois* bought up country seats from impoverished nobles, but commerce and industry continued to be their main sources of income and ultimately of power. The *bourgeois* of France had been investing in land since the sixteenth century, and in the eighteenth a technological revolution in agriculture which increased annual yields made financial returns greater than ever before and attracted substantial amounts of new capital. The speculative enterprise of the *bourgeois* was thus not limited to trade and industry; they had begun to take possession of the noble's traditional inheritance, his estates.

As long as the authority of the aristocracy had been clothed in a religious mantle and the dignity of custom, the *bourgeois* could be kept in their place. But the eighteenth-century nobility, whose personal conduct set the irreligious tone of the age, had divested themselves of their most sacred armor. The noble privileges which persisted in law no longer had any rational or moral justification for the politically conscious among the *bourgeois*. Many had read the contemporary philosophers and knew that an idle class, fulfilling no function in society, was contrary to the natural order. Hence they were no longer content to endure disparagement, to be looked down upon by men whose elevated status they did not respect, especially since many nobles themselves no longer believed in their own right to homage. Young noble blood had joined the American Revolution to fight for liberty and equality, and irreligious Masonic societies were crowded with princes.

Titles, superannuated parchments kept in gothic châteaux, do they bestow upon those who have inherited them the right to aspire to the most distinguished offices in the Church, in the court, in the judiciary or in the army, without their having any of the talents necessary to fulfill them worthily? Because noble warriors once contributed, at the risk of their lives, to the conquest of a kingdom or to the pillage of provinces should their descendants believe that, after so many centuries, they still are entitled to maltreat their vassals? [2]

Thus reasoned the philosopher Baron d'Holbach (1723–1789), mouthpiece of the upper *bourgeois:* nor did any contemporary offer to rebut the argument.

Memoirs and autobiographies of *bourgeois* lawyers who were later among the great tribunes of the French Revolution reveal that they never forgave the slights from nobles which they had suffered in their youth. Chateaubriand (1768–1848) wrote:

This resentment of the *bourgeoisie* against the nobility, which burst forth with such great violence at the moment of the revolution, did not derive from inequality in office; it derived from inequality in esteem. There was no baronet so petty that he did not have the privilege of insulting and disdaining the *bourgeois* to the point of refusing to cross swords with him; the name noble gentleman dominated everything.[3]

The *bourgeois* and their lawyers were the protagonists of the Great Revolution, not because of their suffering at the hands of the state, but because they had grown rich and self-confident and were becoming impatient with the existing regime. The state, which had spent itself in a long series of wars and in the distribution of millions in noble sinecures, was bankrupt and had to rely upon them to raise loans. In the reorganization which was patently inevitable in the last decades of the century, the great *bourgeois* saw the opportunity to achieve political power and prestige commensurate

[2] Baron Paul d'Holbach, *Ethocratie ou le Gouvernement fondé sur la morale* (Amsterdam, 1776), pp. 43–44.

[3] Quoted from Hervé Clérel, comte de Tocqueville, *Histoire philosophique de la règne de Louis XV* (Paris, 1847), II, 42.

with their economic status in the realm. And it was the middle-class lawyers who did the talking during the Revolution as the men of letters in the mid-eighteenth century had done the thinking for the *bourgeois*. The bankers and entrepreneurs themselves could not foretell the direction of the Revolution, and it held many fatal surprises in store for them. Nevertheless the French Revolution can truly be called *bourgeois*, less because it was a plot of the third estate to seize the government than because, after the guillotined heads were buried and the rubble swept away, the *bourgeois* emerged with their rights validated in law, elevated in public consideration, and strengthened in power—goals for which they had been striving for a century.

Last Attempts at Governmental Reform

In the last decades of the old regime there were two major attempts to reform and to reorganize the administration of the French kingdom, the first by a native French administrator, economist, and philosopher, Turgot (1727–1781), the second by a Swiss banker, Necker (1732–1804). Turgot wanted to rationalize the whole administrative system; to abolish sinecures and lavish allowances for the nobility; to economize; to keep within the budget; to abolish provincial restrictions and permit the free movement of grain throughout the length and breadth of the land in order to allay the pangs of hunger during local crop failures; to put an end to forced labor by the peasants on public works; to destroy the monopoly of the guilds which stifled large-scale manufacturing. But the nobles militantly resisted the innovations and Turgot was dismissed.

At first Necker tried to be more persuasive and diplomatic where Turgot had been blunt in proposing his revolutionary changes. In January 1781, however, he embarked upon a novel administrative procedure which shook the pillars of the kingdom far more violently than had any of Turgot's schemes. In imitation of the annual account presented to the English Parliament, he published 100,000 copies of the French national budget, which he called a *Compte Rendu*. For the first time the mystery of the monarchy's finances was revealed to anyone who could read. Though workers and peasants would not buy or read it, the *bourgeois* did. Necker's comments on money grants, pensions, and annual bounties to nobles were hardly circumspect: "Even Your Majesty was amazed to find that on this account your finances were annually charged with near 28,000,000 of *livres*. I much question whether all the Sovereigns in Europe put together lay out in pensions more than one half of the above sum." [4] When describing the countless impediments to free commerce raised by local tolls and prohibitions and the uneven burdens of taxation carried by the various estates, he concluded: "It must be allowed that all this part of our constitution is barbarous." His remedy was in part the same as Turgot's: "It would be a plan as simple as it is grand to render the interior circulation of commerce absolutely free. . . ." [5] But the Minister who had dared to affront the nobility had to go the way of his reforming predecessor.

The French nobility of the eighteenth century is an archetype of a ruling class debilitated by its own uselessness. The men of the court showed themselves weaklings in battle and were distinguished only for their spectacular games at Ver-

[4] *State of the Finances of France Laid before the King, by Mr. Necker Director-General of Finances in the Month of January, 1781*, tr. from the Paris edition (London, 1781), pp. 26–27.

[5] *Ibid.*, p. 92.

sailles. The country nobles who remained smugly on their estates were generally despised. The nobility was incapable of political action beyond backstairs resistance to the efforts of rationalist ministers of state such as Turgot or Necker and hamstringing royal intendants in the provinces. The reforming ministers might have rendered the extinction of the French nobility less precipitate, less bloody. Doomed it had been since the late Middle Ages by the growth of a capitalist system of enterprise which became a great source of wealth and power in the state and had little use for those military attributes cherished by the nobles in the centuries of fighting that had created France. Since capitalism was expanding without significant participation by the nobles, they came to be regarded by the more active elements in the nation as purely decorative, a senseless encumbrance to the economic and political development of France. Nevertheless, a crisis in the French government might have been avoided by reform in the organization of taxation and expenditures, and the transition to *bourgeois* monarchy or to a republic might have been more gradual, smooth, and peaceful if the nobility had been able to merge with the rival groups thirsting for power in the state—the lawyers, the manufacturers, the merchants, and the financiers. But such an amalgamation, partially effected in England, did not take place in France.

CHAPTER V

The British System ⌇⌇⌇⌇⌇⌇

THE *English* are the only people upon earth who have been able to prescribe limits to the power of kings by resisting them; and who, by a series of struggles, have at last establish'd that wise Government, where the Prince is all powerful to do good, and at the same time is restrain'd from committing evil; where the Nobles are great without insolence, tho' there are no Vassals; and where the People share in the Government without confusion.[1]

With such superlatives Voltaire eulogized the British constitution in *Letters Concerning the English Nation* (1733). His compatriot, the Baron de Montesquieu (1689–1755), in his epoch-making *Spirit of the Laws* (1748), was no less enthusiastic about the merits of the system of checks and balances in government and the virtues of what he considered a true separation of the executive, the legislative, and the judicial powers.

Most foreign visitors, of course, had only casual acquaintance with the mechanics of British electioneering for Parliament. Even though they were aware that members took bribes, as noble Roman senators had before them, they did

[1] François Marie Arouet de Voltaire, *Letters Concerning the English Nation* (London, 1733), p. 53.

not consider the evil grave enough to outweigh the manifold excellences of the British system. Recent studies show that about half of a typical mid-century House of Commons consisted of crown dependents—ministers and civil servants, holders of civilian sinecures, court officials, army and navy officers, government contractors, and secret service pensioners. Of the other half, most were hand-picked representatives of the local gentry of the counties. Yet the customary system of patronage, the "rotten boroughs," and the rampant bribery cannot obscure the historic worth of this legislative body without parallel in the Europe of its day. Parliament had chosen the dynasty which ruled over the British Empire and Parliament was sovereign. However corrupt it may be made out to be, it was there, another source of real power in the realm besides the crown. In 1699 William III's Dutch guards had been sent home and standing armies abolished; the King was henceforward dependent for his upkeep and protection upon annual grants from Parliament. The very fact that he had to pack the Parliament with his own placemen to get the legislation he wanted highlights the power of this assembly.

The House of Commons was not a popular democratic assembly in any nineteenth-century sense of the term; but it was an important meeting place for spokesmen of the landed gentry and the moneyed interests to debate the problems of the kingdom. Workers and peasants were not considered responsible members of the body politic, and the issue of their representation was not seriously raised until the agitation aroused by John Wilkes in the seventies. Nevertheless, no one was barred from sitting in the House of Commons because of his class, not even a man who had once been a manual laborer.

The Landed Gentry and the Merchants

While there were remnants of mediaevalism in the English system of land tenure, any man, whatever his origins, could buy and hold land. Merchants who became wealthy acquired country estates and sent their sons to the House of Commons, where, along with the nobility and the upper clergy in the House of Lords, they directed the conduct of the nation's affairs. Merchants who were ennobled were quickly assimilated, and after a generation or two their lowly origin was almost forgotton. Unlike the continental practice which provided all heirs with a title, the English system of primogeniture created among the nobility a class of younger sons who did not bear their father's title and were thus closer in social status to the nonnoble moneyed class of merchants. Younger sons of lords or country gentlemen could enter trade without disparagement. Daniel Defoe, the prolific contemporary pamphleteer, wrote in 1726:

As so many of our noble and wealthy families . . . are raised by and derived from trade, so it is true . . . that many of the younger branches of our gentry, and even of the nobility itself, have descended again into the spring from whence they flowed, and have become tradesmen. . . . Trade is the readiest way for men to raise their fortunes and families; and therefore it is a field for men of figure and of good families to enter upon.[2]

England was in effect governed by a Whig aristocracy of recent and common origin which did not consider the amassing of a fortune in factory or mine or trade with America and India a degradation. The Whig landed gentry were dominant in the Parliament, but the men who came to sit in

[2] Daniel Defoe, *The Complete English Tradesman*, in *Novels and Miscellaneous Works* (Oxford, 1841), XVII, 242-243.

Westminster were in no sense representatives of a land interest in opposition to a commercial interest. Most parliamentary discussions concerned financial and commercial problems: the National Debt, the Sinking Fund, the system of trade bounties and protective duties, the excise, and subsidies for continental armies. All ruling elements in Britain recognized her as a commercial empire and contrasted her maritime character with the military land power of France. The British navy and British commerce were "like Twins . . . born together, and not to live asunder." [3] In 1764 Thomas Whately, a Joint Secretary to the Treasury, wrote: "But happily for this Country the Real and Substantial, and those are the Commercial Interests of Great Britain, are now preferred to every other Consideration. . . ." [4]

There were of course important groups in England who did not enjoy equality in public affairs: the Dissenters, for instance, who refused to join the Church of England. Members of the nonconformist sects enjoyed toleration, however, and though public offices were denied them and the universities were closed to them, they were not prevented from participating in the striving for wealth. They spent their worldly energies in labor, and practiced a thrift bordering on avarice. Their accumulated capital became one of the great resources of the Industrial Revolution.

Local Administration

Unlike most eighteenth-century monarchies on the continent, in England there was no vast nation-wide system of

[3] Daniel Defoe, *A Plan of the English Commerce* (London, 1728), p. 150.

[4] Thomas Whately, *The Regulations Lately Made Concerning the Colonies, and the Taxes Imposed upon Them, Considered* (London, 1765), p. 3.

local administration and justice directed from a central authority. In addition to reasons imbedded in the long development of the British constitution, the compactness of the island may have obviated the need for the elaboration of such a great state bureaucracy. No local organization for the raising of troops under crown control was required since there was little fear of military invasion. Governmental changes could not be effected by the promulgation of royal decrees, and an act of Parliament was necessary before the executive could extend its functions. Local administration was not in the hands of a professional class, such as the French lawyers, but was only an incidental responsibility of the landed gentry, who acted with great independence at the quarter sessions. The administration of the Poor Law, which was solely an obligation of the parishes, gave the local gentry powerful instruments of control over the overwhelming number of inhabitants within their jurisdiction.

Although some complacent English contemporaries like the jurist William Blackstone (1723–1780) upheld England's system of justice as a model, it sanctioned many barbaric punishments. The procedure of appeal from local justice to a higher court, known as certiorari, imposed some uniform judicial practices and kept local authorities within bounds, but there was still great latitude for individual judgment and also for tyrannical abuse. The common law was often cruel and the squire who was justice of the peace often ignorant and arbitrary. Even in the great city of London, Bow Street court proceedings under a Justice Thrasher were hardly more elevated. "To speak the truth plainly, the justice was never indifferent in a cause but when he could get nothing on either side," wrote Henry Fielding (1707–1754) in his novel *Amelia,* where he presents his satirical "observations on the excellency of the English constitution and curious examinations before a justice of the peace." [5] Fielding himself was a Bow Street magistrate and he knew the corruption whereof he spoke. Yet despite all the imperfections of British justice, there was an independent higher judiciary for appeals from the decisions of local magistrates, and the right of habeas corpus often prevented unwarranted prison detentions. To the middle class who were creating England's wealth, the law gave security in the possession of their property and the enjoyment of personal freedom. Of course the poor could rarely avail themselves of the protection of the law, because they had no access to the growing class of lawyers and bondsmen. But with all its worst imperfections, English justice, both in concept and application, set a goal for the rest of the civilized world.

Toward the Industrial Revolution

After 1760, England underwent that acceleration of tempo in all phases of economic life which, since the French economist Auguste Blanqui coined the term in 1837, has been called the Industrial Revolution. This does not mean that there was an abrupt switch from the earlier ways of producing goods and earning a livelihood. There was, however, an intensification in the rate of change; inventions and improvements were multiplied; machinery was more widely applied to manufacturing processes previously done by hand; and new forms for the organization of work were developed. The basic character of the English economy was altered; it became evident that England's wealth was no longer founded primarily upon agriculture, but upon the manufacture and

[5] Henry Fielding, *Amelia* (1751). Quoted from the Everyman's Library edition (London, 1930), I, 7.

exchange of industrial products. Arthur Young noted in 1770 that the inhabitants of England and Wales were no longer overwhelmingly agricultural. This was his curious breakdown of the sources of livelihood for the total population:

Agriculture	2,800,000
Landlords, mines, etc.	800,000
Manufactures	3,000,000
Commerce	700,000
Non-industrious poor	500,000
Clergy, law, etc. etc.	200,000
By public revenue [army, navy, civil servants]	500,000 [6]

A number of circumstances in English economic and social life were conducive to this great outburst of activity. Political stability had favored the accumulation of capital, while the prestige which commerce and industry enjoyed encouraged investment in productive undertakings. A spirit of enterprise animated the nation, and men of imagination who planned novel projects or wished to exploit a promising invention found ready backing among English investors. Contemporaries were impressed with the spectacle of men risking their fortunes on all sorts of new devices. "The age is running mad after innovation," grunted Dr. Samuel Johnson (1709–1784), "all the business of the world is to be done in a new way; men are to be hanged in a new way; Tyburn itself is not safe from the fury of innovation." [7]

The regulations governing guilds and corporations had survived, but they were regarded rather lightly as old-

---

[6] Arthur Young, *A Six Months Tour through the North of England* (London, 1770), IV, 569.

[7] Quoted from T. S. Ashton, *The Industrial Revolution, 1760–1830* (London, 1948), p. 11.

fashioned prohibitions and their violators were rarely prosecuted. Naturally enough, the more rapid industrial developments occurred in those unincorporated towns which had never been under mediaeval restrictions against new manufacturing processes and labor practices and in those areas which enjoyed special exemptions. As a generality, in England men were less subject to ordinances which impeded economic progress than anywhere in Europe.

England's trade with the colonies, which by 1775 amounted to about a third of her foreign commerce, had increased six times in volume from 1700 to the outbreak of the American Revolution. Exports to the colonies had reached four and a half million pounds sterling, and imports from the colonies more than five million pounds sterling. England's total overseas trade more than quadrupled in the course of the century. The rising demand obviously gave manufacturers and large-scale farmers incentive to expand their operations and improve their products.

England's happy combination of human and natural resources helped to create a new technology affecting both the quality and quantity of output, as well as the organization of labor in field and factory. Her navigable waters and outlets to the sea facilitated both interior and foreign commerce; her rivers supplied power to drive machinery; and her abundant coal and iron gave her the products basic to most industrial processes. Moreover, she had men of talent and energy who knew how to utilize these natural advantages. The spirit of intellectual inquiry which was burgeoning everywhere in Europe had taken firmest root in England. Chemists like Joseph Priestley (1733–1804) and Joseph Black (1728–1799) conducted experiments whose results had wide practical application in British industry. Sometimes the scientists themselves became inventors and pioneer manufacturers.

The publications of the Royal Society of London, the research of the scientific laboratories, especially those of the Scottish universities, the ingenuity of a group of practical-minded inventors, and the daring of entrepreneurs were all contributory elements in the process of altering the industrial face of England. There was mobility in this English society. Manufacturers, inventors, and scientists discussed common interests and problems in associations such as the Lunar Society of Birmingham, to which the famous pottery manufacturer Josiah Wedgwood (1730–1795), the inventor James Watt (1736–1819), and the Birmingham industrialist Matthew Boulton (1728–1809) all belonged. Ideas were generated at these meetings and partnerships were formed to exploit them.

There was a new interest in improving transportation. Highways were broadened and their surfaces improved to accommodate a large volume of traffic in any weather. It was an age of canal building. In 1761 the Duke of Bridgewater built a canal to connect his coal mines at Worsley with the town of Manchester seven miles away, and the relatively cheap transportation by water enabled him to undersell all his competitors. In the next quarter century new waterways were opened until England was literally covered with a network of canals.

In agriculture, although new methods and techniques were not widely adopted throughout the land, the groundwork was laid for the accelerated developments of the next century. The practice of scientific husbandry by rich landholders became such a craze that even George III prided himself on being called the farmer-king. Wealthy noblemen and squires like the famous Coke of Holkham (1752–1842) occupied themselves with the reclamation of fens and marshes. Following the lead of Robert Bakewell (1725–1794), they bred livestock for better and more meat. And Viscount Charles Townshend (1674–1738), known as "Turnip Townshend," showed them the virtues of a four-crop rotation system which alternated arable farming with the production of turnips and clover, to provide winter fodder for livestock and at the same time to replenish the fertility of the soil.

The Mechanical Inventions

The augmented number of mechanical inventions registered by the Commissioners of Patents reflects the accelerating pace of the Industrial Revolution. While prior to 1760 more than a dozen patents were rarely awarded in any one year, in 1766 the number rose to thirty-one, and in 1769 to thirty-six; in 1783 there was a sudden increase to 64; then followed a decline until another spurt brought it to 85 in the year 1792. The technological revolution was already gaining momentum in the last decades of the eighteenth century, although it was the next quarter century that saw a tremendous bound forward, with 250 patented inventions for the year 1825 alone. Broadly speaking, the early improvements in spinning, weaving, and mining were labor-saving devices which made it possible to maintain production with a limited work force. In many instances, children could be trained at the new machines to perform jobs which had formerly been set for men and women. In the last decades of the century, when labor was more plentiful, inventors concentrated on increasing output.

Machinery was already in use by 1700 for such heavy

tasks as sawing lumber and hammering metal, and for some lighter jobs such as coin stamping, but simple tools and manually supplied power were still the rule for most manufacturing processes. During the course of the century, and particularly in its second half, many more machines were introduced in metallurgy, pottery making, and textiles.

There were some technological improvements in the mining of coal and output increased from two and a half million tons in 1700 to three and three quarter million tons in 1750 to ten million tons in 1800. The most important invention, widely used by 1760, was Thomas Newcomen's atmospheric engine, which pumped the water out of the pits and enabled the miners to work the deeper mineral deposits. Other improvements, such as the laying of iron-track wagonways, made it possible to use less human and animal power in hauling coal, both in the galleries of the pits and above ground to waterways and industrial establishments. The greatest expansion in coal mining came in the next century, and it is likely that the relatively slow progress of this industry in the eighteenth set limits to the expansion of manufactures requiring this basic fuel for power.

The iron industry was stimulated by the demand for munitions, and its production increased from 20,000 tons in 1740 to 156,000 tons in 1800. Abraham Darby and his son had freed the iron industry from its dependence on rapidly thinning woodlands by substituting coke for charcoal in smelting ore into pig iron and in converting pig into the cast iron suitable for pots and pans and some types of ordnance. The forging of wrought iron, a less brittle and purer metal used in cutlery and nails, still required charcoal until Henry Cort in 1784 patented a puddling, or stirring, process. This method separated from the liquid metal the carbon impurities which had previously interfered with the use of coke in making wrought iron. Cort's roller patent further provided a means of fashioning the iron bars into plates and rods.

Under the impetus supplied by men like Matthew Boulton, England became the foremost producer of metal wares in the world, famous for Birmingham hardware and Sheffield silver plate. The metal manufacturers employed water wheels and eventually the steam engine to supply power for their flatting mills which beat ingots into sheets, for their coin making machines, lathes, grinders, and polishers. In this manner costs were reduced until Protestant England was making crucifixes for the Catholic countries of Europe at a wholesale price equivalent to fifteen cents a dozen.

Boulton's initiative, combined with the inventive genius of James Watt, revolutionized not only the production of metal goods, but of all English industry, by replacing water power with steam. Watt's steam engine had been patented in 1769, but its manufacture had been retarded by a shortage of skilled workmen who could make cylinders to such exact specifications that from end to end they would accommodate smoothly the pistons whose plunging strokes were the source of power. Watt formed a partnership with Boulton in 1774, and at their Soho plant workers and engineers were assembled, production difficulties ironed out, and the steam engine was equipped with rotary parts to turn shafts and drive powerful machines. The problem of boring cylinders of precise dimensions had been solved by adapting the cannon borer developed by "iron mad" John Wilkinson (who carried his fetish to the point of building an iron coffin for himself).

In the pottery works of Staffordshire, the use of water- or steam-driven mixing and grinding machines, potter's wheels, and presses to squeeze clay into molds contributed to the growth of an industry which sold English "china" to every country of Europe and to the colonies. In his pottery works at Etruria, Josiah Wedgwood invented or perfected tools, lathes, coloring processes; substituted steam for water power; and introduced novelties in the organization and supervision of his workers. His *objets d'art*, as well as the ordinary household wares on which he concentrated, were of a quality to please even the Tsarina of all the Russias.

The most widespread development of the Industrial Revolution in the eighteenth century occurred in textiles, and by 1800 hundreds of mills on the river banks of Lancashire and Yorkshire were manufacturing yarn with water-power driven machines. Few changes were made in the weaving of cloth. John Kay in 1733 invented a flying shuttle which was knocked across a wide loom by hammers instead of being passed by hand from one worker to another, but the invention was bitterly opposed by the weavers, who feared the loss of their jobs, and its adoption was delayed. Similarly, Edmund Cartwright's automatic power loom (1785) found no ready acceptance until the nineteenth century. Indeed, there was little incentive to speed up weaving until the spinning processes had been improved, since it took anywhere from four to ten spinners to prepare yarn for a single loom. The gap was bridged by a number of inventions in the spinning of textile yarns, of which the first was Thomas Lombe's silk-throwing machine (1718), which stepped up the production of silk yarn. A more dramatic change in spinning was the water frame (1768) patented by Richard Arkwright, a wigmaker and barber whose invention brought him fame, fortune, and ennoblement. Ark-wright's device employed rollers, driven by water power, to draw out the fibers into loose bands which were then passed to the spindles for twisting. The end product, a coarse yarn suitable for cotton textiles, was manufactured in far greater quantities than had been possible with manu-ally fed spindles. At about the same time, James Hargreaves invented a jenny (named for his wife) which could spin a hundred threads of yarn at once by means of several spindles vertically installed. The jenny did not require an elaborate power wheel to drive it and could be operated by hand in a worker's home, but the yarn it produced was weak and easily broken. In 1779 Samuel Crompton combined the features of the water frame and the spinning jenny in a mule (so-called because of its hybrid character), which was both water driven and could at the same time spin multiple threads of fine, strong yarn. Improvements in bleaching and dyeing and in printing patterns on cloth through the use of rollers were also introduced in the last quarter of the century. As a consequence of this accumulation of inven-tions, England easily dominated the textile markets of the world. By 1800 the ordinary Englishman could afford to wear cotton underclothing which a century before had been the prerogative of the rich.

The Factory System

The growth of the factory system was the most striking social and organizational aspect of the Industrial Revolution. There were a number of reasons which moved employers to draw personnel to one place of work whenever possible. Smelting and rolling in the iron industry was not profitable on a small scale in dispersed units. In the cotton industry a single water wheel or a steam engine in a factory could supply power for many operatives. Workers in the new chemical and machine-manufacturing industries required strict supervision, which could best be provided in a single locale. In pottery works, such as those of Josiah Wedgwood, a large agglomeration of workers greatly facilitated the sub-division of labor. The concentration of workers in a single establishment made it possible to stop thefts of raw material during the manufacture of woolens, a frequent abuse under the old putting-out system. The factory system brought with it a new regimen for workers—symbolized by the gong —which was absent both in agriculture and in domestic handicraft. This organizational novelty and its effect upon workers proved in the long run to be as revolutionary in its consequences as the technological improvements themselves.

In the early period of the Industrial Revolution the labor supply in the towns was far from plentiful. Unless they were forced by hunger, workers were usually reluctant to seek jobs in factories where they had to surrender their freedom to a strict discipline alien to the cottager. Generally the ancient Elizabethan Poor Law militated against the move-ment of workers from one area to another, for if a man left his native parish and stayed away for a year there was no longer a local obligation to support him in time of need. Hence the importance of children in the labor force during this period. In many districts overseers of the poor, in order to get rid of their charges, especially the foundlings, and to ease the tax burden of the parish, transferred them in batches to the cotton masters of the north. The sufferings of these children, apprenticed in factories where they worked twelve to fifteen hours a day, have been poignantly depicted in testimony delivered before contemporary Parliamentary

Commissions studying factory legislation. Recent apologists for the early factory system have this to say about the "hell of human cruelty" in which the children spent their lives: that it was probably not much worse than the condition of foundlings under the previous practice of local apprenticeship.

The sizable labor force employed in the construction of capital equipment such as machines and factories and on the improvements of transport meant fewer workers available for the production of consumer goods—cloths, foodstuffs, furniture—at the very time when there was a substantial increase in the population of Britain. With the exception of pottery, practically all items destined for the ultimate user were in short supply. Hence after the middle of the century there was a sharp over-all price rise, about 30 per cent from the middle fifties to the early nineties, followed by a precipitous jump of 100 per cent during the following quarter century. Wages by no means kept pace with this general price rise. During periods of commercial depression there was great suffering among the industrial workers, a condition with which the old Poor Law, providing local responsibility for those who belonged to the parish, could not cope. Working class revolt was sporadic, inchoate, and violent. Strikes and outbursts of machine-breaking—that primitive, instinctive reaction of hate among workers—were repressed with brutality.

The Pattern of Trade

Though the area of wheat under cultivation in the eighteenth century was enlarged by about a third and the yield per acre raised by about a tenth, the growth of population was so marked after 1770 that Britain became an importer of grains in most years. Toward the end of the century, as the new factories poured forth manufactured goods in ever greater quantities, Britain came to rely significantly upon foreign, especially European, markets for their disposal The basic modern pattern of Great Britain's import-export trade was established during this period. From the colo nies she received raw cotton, tobacco, sugar, and spices, sending in exchange cloth, hardware, glass, books, beer, snuff, slippers, and slaves transported from Africa. She ex- ported to Europe her textiles, swords, cutlery, pottery, paper and glass manufactures; and she imported wine, fruit, oil, and wool from southern Europe; naval stores, lumber, metals, and flax (used for sails) from northern and Baltic Europe; some manufactured luxuries from Italy, France, and Germany. England thus became a unique type of national workshop dependent for her very existence upon the importation of an increasing proportion of food and raw materials from abroad and upon the capacity of other countries in the world to buy her manufactured products.

CHAPTER VI

Empire of the Hapsburgs

THE Austro-Hungarian Empire of the nineteenth century —a relatively effective government—was in large measure a product of eighteenth-century administrative reform. During the long reigns of the Empress Maria Theresa and her son Joseph II, attempts were made to integrate the disparate land areas of the Hapsburg Empire in central Europe into a Danubian kingdom. No real national unity in an English or a French sense was ever achieved, nor was an Austro-Hungarian personality created; hence the destiny of this empire was ultimate dissolution. Nevertheless, the judicial, administrative, and social reforms, both those inaugurated with caution by Maria Theresa and those pushed through impetuously by Joseph, did succeed in curbing the centrifugal forces at play in the component states of the Hapsburg Empire. They established an initial pattern of administrative centralism and uniformity of procedure which helped to keep this loose-jointed structure together until the First World War.

Under Charles VI (1711–1740) the Hapsburg Empire was a mere agglomeration of territories loosely united in a personal union with the monarch. A Hapsburg was traditionally elected Holy Roman Emperor; in addition to this

office each of the hereditary possessions of the dynasty carried with it a separate title: the Hapsburg was Archduke of
Austria, King of Bohemia, Apostolic King of Hungary. In
the two mediaeval kingdoms, Hungary with a population of
7,000,000 and Bohemia with 3,000,000, the nobles had retained extensive autonomous rights and privileges. They had
independent diets and each Hapsburg heir was crowned
separately in Buda and in Prague. Before the death of
Charles VI the diets of the constituent territories had accepted a Pragmatic Sanction whereby they agreed, in order
to keep the empire together, to recognize his daughter Maria
Theresa as ruler of the several kingdoms, since he had no
male issue. But despite the promises—in which the great
foreign powers joined—the actual coronations of the new
Queen did not run smoothly. The Czech and Magyar no-
bilities would not readily swear fealty to a woman. The
legitimacy of Maria Theresa's succession was the origin of
a European war during which Prussia, France, Bavaria, and
minor German states tried to partition the lands of the
House of Hapsburg. This War of the Austrian Succession
(1740–1748) was the external shock which gave immediate
impetus to plans for the unification of a Danubian Empire.
It became clear to Maria Theresa and her advisers that the
House of Hapsburg must either proceed to integrate its
hereditary possessions or face dismemberment.

In 1741, in the early stages of the war, Charles Albert,
elector of Bavaria and pretender to the crown of the Holy
Roman Empire, forced his way into Prague and was ac-
claimed king of Bohemia before an assembly of four hundred
nobles in the Cathedral of St. Vitus. When Maria Theresa
retrieved the crown of Bohemia two years later as the fortunes of war turned, she had it transferred physically to

Vienna, a symbol of her determination to prevent any further disaffection among the Bohemian nobility. Their contumacy was punished in a set of administrative orders issued over the next decades which completely altered the relations of the central government with the Bohemians. There was a frank invasion of the autonomous rights which had been guaranteed them in the seventeenth century. In 1749 the chancellery of Bohemia was merged with the central chancellery of the empire. The diet of Bohemia had to surrender its control over provincial administration and the native army. Bohemia was ultimately subjected to an Austrian code of law and judicial appeals had to be taken to Vienna. The German language was made compulsory in schools and offices and the effort to eradicate distinctive Bohemian identity was intensified.

In 1741 the diet of the Hungarian magnates, though they did not welcome an invader as had a large body of the Bohemian nobles, took advantage of Maria Theresa's military weakness to insist upon the reaffirmation of their franchises: immunity from taxation, freedom from Hapsburg administrative control, the reservation of offices in Hungary to Magyars. During protracted negotiations, the Queen appealed to every mediaeval chivalric and contemporary sentimental emotion of the assembled nobles. She presented a spectacle of weeping beauty in distress, displayed her infant son, wore mourning clothes topped by the ancient crown of Hungary. In the end, after much unromantic haggling, she ratified most of the privileges of the nobility; in exchange she received 100,000 troops for the war with Prussia and, the story runs, heard the cry, "*Moriamur pro rege nostro Maria Theresa.*"

A temporary entente was thus effected between the imperial ruler of the Hapsburgs and the "high table" of the nobility of Hungary. The magnates frequented the palace at Vienna, abandoned their distinctive national costumes, learned to speak German, and accepted the titles of prince, count, and baron of the empire which they had previously shunned. Honorific offices and foreign embassies were bestowed upon them to bolster up their pride. An ingenious system of marriages engineered by the crown with consummate skill furthered the assimilation of the Magyar nobility with the Austrians.

During the reign of Maria Theresa the boundaries of Hungary were stretched into Polish territory and new frontier areas in the Balkans were wrested from the feeble Ottoman Empire. In return for imperial benefits conferred, however, the Magyar nobles were constrained ultimately to surrender many of the prerogatives agreed upon in 1741. The diet of Hungary, which according to the Golden Bull of 1222 was supposed to be convoked annually, met only thrice during Maria Theresa's long regime.

The Reforms of Chancellor Haugwitz

In addition to integrating the feudal aristocracy of the two most important states with traditions of independence, Chancellor Count Friedrich Wilhelm Haugwitz effected a general administrative reform throughout the Empire which, as Maria Theresa later wrote his widow, "restored the government from confusion to order." Everywhere this involved extending imperial power and curtailing the privileges of the nobility. It meant rationalizing the tax system so that it provided the revenues necessary for war. It entailed developing the agencies of the central government and curbing the autonomy of local diets and executive committees.

The key battle, as always, was fought over the incidence of taxation. Maria Theresa found an empty treasury when she ascended the throne. By instituting and enforcing a universal system of taxation, from which there were no exemptions, neither of prince nor of lackey, the imperial government freed itself from beggarly dependence upon the state diets. The states were deprived of the revenue from indirect levies on salt and tobacco and from the stamp tax, and they had to present their budgets of income and expenditures to the Chamber of Accounts (*Hofrechnenkammer*) in Vienna for approval. The annual revenue of the empire trebled during Maria Theresa's reign.

In the over-all reorganization, the central state chancellery and the Council of War were granted exclusive jurisdiction in all the Hapsburg territories. Absolute centralization of the army and of foreign affairs pulled the empire through the bitter conflicts with Frederick II. Gradually but relentlessly administrative powers were withdrawn from the permanent committees of the provincial diets which had previously operated as executive bodies between sessions and were vested in the hands of a direct representative of the Empress. The diets themselves, on the rare occasions when they met, were reduced to the level of formal assemblies whose main order of business was to vote the demands of the crown. Imperial functionaries moved freely throughout the administrative system of the separate states, into areas where they had never before penetrated. As agents of the crown, they could, at least in principle, hear appeals from the peasants over the heads of their lords.

Though there was continuity to the long-range policy of the Hapsburg administrators, a number of whom bridged the reign of the Empress, the coregency, and the independent reign of Joseph II, the tempers of the two monarchs and their methods of operation diverged radically. Maria Theresa's tactics can be described as the iron hand in a velvet glove (*douce violence*); her son charged ahead like a bull, despite opposition and criticism. Defeat in war at the hands of Frederick II of Prussia, who had robbed her of Silesia because she had neither the money nor the organization to support a military defense of the Hapsburg lands, forced the Empress to resolve upon a number of antifeudal measures and restrictions on the temporal power of the church. She was nonetheless a pious Catholic and by no means a beacon of the Enlightenment. She understood the requirements of effective absolutism based on the clear supremacy of the sovereign over all classes and the necessity of obtaining a maximum contribution for the support of the dynastic state from nobles, peasants, and churchmen alike. Yet her reforms were moderate and limited in their scope. Though she imposed state officials over the feudal nobles to guide, direct, and tax them, she still accepted the old class hierarchy of peasants under the control of their lords.

At the time of Maria Theresa's accession, the peasants had the status of mediaeval serfs; they could neither leave the land, nor marry, nor bring up their children in new occupations without prior permission of their local lords. They were subject to a host of servitudes covered by the Slavic word *robot* (work). Under the Empress's reforms, while the legal position of the serfs remained fundamentally the same, manorial dues owed their lords were lightened. In Bohemia she broke up her own extensive crown domains and sold the land to the peasants; in both Austria and Bohemia she made inroads into the system of serfdom by establishing royal commissions which at least fixed and entered upon written protocols the manorial dues which a serf owed —a measure of protection from a lord's caprice and limitless exactions.

A royal patent of 1773 alleviating the peasants' burden of road work in Bohemia resulted in an uprising which only confirmed the Empress in her policy of relative moderation, despite her son's chafing at the bit to institute a vast peasant reform. The decree was misinterpreted by the peasants as a general emancipation from all manorial dues and during the wild peasant rebellion which followed, châteaux were pillaged and an imperial army had to save Prague from hordes of serfs marching on the capital. Humbling the Bohemian nobility while at the same time preserving the basis of the ancient system of land tenure was a precarious balance to maintain.

By a patent of 1749 justice was separated from administration and the prospect of judicial reforms throughout the empire was raised. Law in the Hapsburg lands was a potpourri of local custom, Roman civil law, canon law, and imperial ordinances. Men were judged by different standards, depending upon their status in society. Punishments were barbaric: mutilation, branding, and the wheel. A special commission set up in 1767 studied the possibility of promulgating a common legal code for Austria, Hungary, and Bohemia; but after long inquiries the specific results incorporated in the criminal code of 1770—the *Nemesis Teresiana* —were for the most part limited to the abolition of some of the more cruel forms of punishment and the elimination of crimes such as sorcery. In time similar imperial commissions were multiplied to cover many aspects of social and political life, though their proposals were rarely carried through with success. The Chastity Commission, designed to prevent illegitimate love-making, was one of the Empress's less felicitous innovations.

Maria Theresa subscribed to the principle that education was within the province of the state, that it was a political matter. Universities and secondary schools were therefore placed under her control, and the state dictated the entrance requirements and the curriculum. At the same time, primary education was emancipated from the church. Though Frederick II called her an "apostolic hag," Maria Theresa's religion did not allow for papal interference in the ecclesiastical affairs of her empire. Bishops were prohibited from corresponding directly with Rome, and in 1773 she joined the rest of Catholic Europe in suppressing the Jesuit Order.

The contemporary publicist Joseph von Sonnenfels (1732–1817), who had been one of the intellectual proponents of reform, wrote in eulogy of his Empress:

At the advent of Maria Theresa the monarchy was without influence abroad, without strength at home; . . . agriculture was in a wretched state; commerce mediocre; finance without direction or credit. At her death she transmitted to her successor a state improved by her reforms and raised to the level which the greatness, fertility, and the intelligence of its inhabitants should have assured it.[1]

Joseph II: Absolutist Reformer

Joseph II, who had been quarreling with his mother over matters of state policy throughout their long core-

[1] Louis Léger, *Histoire de l'Autriche Hongrie* (Paris, 1920), p. 368.

gency (1765–1780), drove the Theresian reforms to their logical and rational conclusion. He strove to outdo Frederick II of Prussia in creating an absolutism with uniform rules and practices founded on what he considered the principles of reason, in defiance of any religious and historical traditions however powerful or deep-rooted. His doctrinaire approach is well illustrated in his uncompromising Germanization policy. To a Magyar noble who had remonstrated with him, he replied:

Every plea must be supported by irrefutable arguments drawn from reason. . . . The German language is the universal tongue of my empire. I am the Emperor of Germany. The states which I possess are provinces which form a single body with the state of which I am the head. If the Kingdom of Hungary were the most important of my possessions, I would not hesitate to impose its language on the other countries.[2]

In the name of his philosophical and étatist principles, Joseph II went far beyond his mother in attacking papal relations with members of the ecclesiastical hierarchy in the empire. In vain did Pope Pius VI travel to Vienna in a forlorn attempt to stem the antipapal movement which later came to be known in the church as Josephinism. To Joseph the very existence of monastic establishments devoted solely to contemplation without work was a violation of rational economics and he suppressed them outright with a decree. This disciple of the French physiocrats tried to eliminate waste in every branch of his economy, and not even the dead were exempt from his regulatory zeal. He decreed against coffins, considering the shroud a sufficient envelopment.

[2] *Ibid.*, p. 371.

Truly revolutionary for an Emperor of the Catholic House of Hapsburg was the Edict of Toleration of 1781, which permitted the private exercise of their religion to Lutherans, Calvinists, and Greek Orthodox Christians. There was some amelioration in the condition of the Jews, to whom a few new occupations were opened. But the broad implications of Joseph's religious toleration should not be exaggerated. He drew the line at deists. If anyone inscribed himself as such he was to receive twenty-four baton blows, not because he was a deist, but because he pretended to be something he knew nothing about.

Joseph II's abolition of serfdom was the most spectacular reform of the whole Age of Reason: his mother had alleviated the burdens of the peasants; he formally emancipated them and bestowed upon them property rights. Joseph dealt with the problem of serfdom in two stages. First, in a series of edicts from 1781 to 1785 he endowed the serfs with legal personality: the peasants of Austria, Hungary, Bohemia, and Transylvania were thereafter at liberty to marry, to migrate, to take employment, and to raise their children in accordance with their own lights without the consent of their manorial lords. Secondly, in the last years of his life, he tackled the problem of providing the freedmen of the empire with land of their own. It has been estimated that before Joseph's reforms, only about 27 per cent of a peasant's income remained for the support of his family after the 10 per cent tithe to the church, the 29 per cent payment to the lord of the manor, and the 34 per cent tax to the state. The emancipation of the serfs had not in and of itself altered their fiscal obligations to the lord and the church. Joseph's policy aimed to reduce these obligations to a single tax which would have left the peasant about 70 per cent of his earnings. The church was dealt with summarily—the tithe simply abolished. In addition to reducing the peasants' dues, the Emperor's decrees provided for the actual purchase of the land they tilled at easy payments. A strong independent peasantry, he hoped, would make the foundation of his new empire. The freedmen, of course, were immediately subjected to Joseph's paternal despotism. He taught them to improve their agricultural techniques, favored the breeding of horses over cattle, and prohibited the peasants from baking gingerbread because it was bad for their stomachs. The final decrees of 1789 which would have given them economic independence were never actually made effective—so violent were the protests and rebellions which overwhelmed the dying monarch.

The new judicial procedures which Joseph instituted were probably the most lasting accomplishments of this zealot who, in the brief decade of his independent reign, tried to alter the whole face of his empire. In 1786, part of a new civil code was promulgated; in 1787, a penal code which abolished the death penalty for many crimes. In effect, Joseph nationalized the judicial system. Only in civil cases was the patrimonial court of the noble still operative. There were peasants' advocates in every province and appeals could be made to officials of the central government. The judicial hierarchy was crowned by a Supreme Court in Vienna which set up legal standards for the whole empire.

Under Joseph the empire was given a symmetrical structure: it was divided into thirteen states, each of which was subdivided into circles. The cities of the empire were stripped of their variegated mediaeval administrative forms and all were placed under similar municipal organizations. As a protectionist, Joseph tried to foster industrial developments on an empire-wide basis which would free his states from reliance on the English and the French for manufactured products such as metal wares and textiles.

Joseph not only compelled provincial communities to build schools: he made secular education compulsory, a requirement which resulted in the highest rate of school attendance in Europe but raised opposition among Catholics, Protestants, and Jews, who dreaded risking their children to his godless system. In his higher education curriculum, the enlightened despot was not too much interested in philosophy and abstract thinking; he favored the practical arts and the medical and juridical faculties. His exclusive admiration for the concrete and the utilitarian makes him appear rather boorish. He could be condescending to Mozart, the greatest creative genius of his age, and complain that one of his operas had "much too many notes."

He lifted the censorship, out of a desire to see the superstitions of the past denounced and to get more taxes from an expanded book-publishing business. He allowed free criticism even of himself. He was the archetype of that bizarre combination of enlightenment and despotism which allowed the world to say what it wished, provided that he could do as he pleased.

In the last years of his life there was a widespread countermovement against his Germanization, his anticlericalism, and his mania for regulations. A rebellion in the Netherlands crushed the spirit of the monarch who could not comprehend the ingratitude of his subjects. His successor gave way on many crucial points on which Joseph with his one-track mind had obdurately insisted. His attempt to mold a nation-state out of the Austro-Hungarian Empire was a dismal failure; it was probably an impossible undertaking. He died a disgruntled imperial philosopher, to whose tyranny of reason men would not submit.

CHAPTER VII

Prussia: The State as Machine〜〜

FREDERICK II in 1740 inherited from his choleric father a small but well-knit, bureaucratic state machine, which
supported a remarkably large and well-trained army. Frederick accepted as his lifework the task of perfecting this
engine of war and of making himself its sole head and di-
rector, its prime mover. He was his own minister of foreign affairs and his own commander in chief of the armies.
While he sought advice from collegiate boards, though not
often from individual civil servants who might thus come
to exercise undue personal influence over him, he allowed
no important decision in the government of the kingdom of
Prussia to be arrived at without being submitted to the prior
scrutiny of the monarch. Here was a centralized administration, a complete bureaucracy, a monolith. Frederick imitated Louis XIV's practices of state organization and improved upon them with such absolutist zeal that the famous:
"I am the State" was more applicable in his kingdom than it
had ever been in the French monarchy. Prussia was small
enough so that, with a tremendous expenditure of energy
and relentless application to the most minute problems of
government, the King personally could supervise the whole

of his domain without being forced to delegate significant authority.

Frederick's concept of the state and his view of the role of the sovereign were set forth with Gallic clarity in his *Political Testament of 1752*, not published in full until after the First World War, so nakedly frank were its revelations of the mainsprings of Prussian power:

A well conducted government ought to have a system as coherent as a system of philosophy, so that all measures are well reasoned, and finance, policy, and the army are coordinated to the same end: namely, the integration of the state and the increase of its power. Now a system can only emanate from a single brain; it must be the sovereign's. Idleness, pleasure-seeking, and imbecility are the causes that keep princes from the noble task of securing the happiness of their people. . . . The sovereign is the first servant of the state.[1]

What is arresting about this first *Testament* is not its formulation of a rationale of government, novel though its principles were, but the fact that this ideal of an autocracy imposed upon the state to further its aggrandizement was actually put into practice during his own and succeeding reigns. His *rêveries politiques*, as he called the daydreams about his dynastic plans, became stark realities, if not in his lifetime, then within a few generations. For more than a hundred and fifty years after his death, his complete identification of the civilian and the military state and the demand for blind obedience to this monster remained embedded in the Prussian character.

Frederick was an animated administrative automaton, an embodiment of the reason of state. It is characteristic that he welcomed to his court the French philosopher Julien de

[1] *Die Politischen Testamente Friedrich's des Grossen*, p. 38.

La Mettrie (1709–1751), the notorious author of *Man the Machine*, and wrote a eulogy upon him after his death. (A passion for food was what these two materialists had in common.) There was a touch of genius in Frederick: he was an intellectual, a poetaster, a flute player, and on occasion a brilliant writer. He was the philosopher-king, immured in his work cabinet, emerging only for his regular inspection tours and to make war with a cold brilliance that has seldom been matched in recorded history. Frederick was a machine, and he created a military nation-state in his own image.

Civil Servants

The Prussian officials, cogs in this bureaucratic machine, were under the continual supervision and suspicion of their master. He evolved an intricate system of spies on his own administrators, and dismissals were frequent. No Prussian bureaucrat had a proprietary sense of security in his office like the French official who had bought his sinecure; the Prussian could be sent to Spandau prison without trial. Officials had to pass stringent examinations after they had gone through courses in "cameralism," that eighteenth-century German equivalent for the precepts of public administration. A recent historian of the eighteenth-century Prussian system has aptly contrasted the training of the Prussian with that of the contemporary French civil servant. While the French official was almost always a lawyer, who thought in terms of the abstractions of Roman law to which the realities of France, pockmarked with feudal remnants, could not be made to conform even under a centralized monarchy, in Prussia the civil servant had studied his native agriculture, knew the prevailing economic ideas, and could cope with financial problems and an accounting system. Since Prussian industry, except for state-sponsored enterprises, was negligible in this period, Frederick's bureaucracy had no rival in attracting the talent of commoners. Though the nobility was favored in the distribution of high office in the state, on all administrative levels aristocrat and commoner were intermingled as they were in contemporary British commercial enterprises. This was one of the great strengths of the system.

The Administrative Structure

The whole administrative structure was built up so that a small state, originally poor in natural resources, could maintain an army continually at war. The Prussian nobles were made into a ruling caste in the army and into responsible administrators on their great landed estates. They were not allowed to become decorative idlers. They had to serve and to govern. The whole of the nobility was in the army on active duty for life. Officers were chosen for high command primarily upon their show of extraordinary ability, their sense of discipline, and their devotion to the sovereign. The army officered by nobles was the core of the state; it became its reason for existence. On the landed estates, especially in the east, the Prussian Junkers were the administrators of the police and of local justice for their peasants. The position of the Junkers was in marked contrast with that of the French nobility, which had been uprooted from the soil. Power over the peasantry was the Junkers' reward for subservience to the Prussian monarch.

Beneath the king, the Prussian central bureaucratic mechanism was controlled by a General Directory of Ministers, who shared responsibility for all decisions. In the provinces the chief agents of the system were the Councilors of Taxes whose function it was to draw as much revenue as possible out of the Prussian economy. Frederick derived his monies from crown lands, woods, mills, subsidies, tithes, ferry-dues, tolls, salt, fisheries, game licenses, stamped paper, registration of deeds, taxes on employment, an excise on all commodities coming into the towns, whether necessities or luxuries, and on all merchandise. In addition, he billeted soldiers and levied fees on those who wished to purchase substitute recruits. Frederick had no use for tax farmers, who took a cut of the royal income, as was the practice in France. He exacted the taxes with the "utmost rigor" but his people did not complain, he maintained, because he collected the revenues in his own name and did not employ secondary extortioners.

Given an ill-favored land with limited potentialities, the Prussian kings tried to balance their budgets and finance their wars by a penny-pinching reduction of expenditures for everything useless. No towns dared to lay out funds for embellishments without royal approval, which was rarely forthcoming. Shrewdly enough, the tax-collecting functions were vested in the same local agency whose officers soberly fostered the improvement of agricultural and industrial techniques. These officials whipped the people into ever-greater feats of production by sheer hard work, in order that Prussia might enjoy a favorable balance of trade and have the necessary bullion to feed the army, which would increase the state's weight in the European equilibrium.

In addition to squeezing the peasants and townspeople, the state itself took the initiative in fully utilizing Prussia's meager resources. Frederick drained swamps, dredged rivers, built roads, and distributed land to ex-soldiers. He established a company, taking most of the shares himself, for foreign trade and shipping. He opened a state bank in 1765. And he sent bureaucrats to England to learn the new industrial techniques and buy machinery for use in the state-owned mines, copper mills, cannon foundries, and saltworks.

A vast output of paper reports kept the Prussian bureaucratic machine going. The reports usually grew out of the collective deliberations of boards and committees, and had an impersonal tone in keeping with the dehumanized character of the administration. In time it was inevitable that this rigid bureaucracy should bog down in its own system. Fear inspired by the monarch who was chief executive became so great that he was often fed information which was pleasing rather than true. As a matter of fact the whole state machine did not render a very brilliant account of itself during the early Napoleonic Wars, when its daemonic head was no longer there to provide the impetus. Nevertheless, for purposes of eighteenth-century warfare it was by far the most effective military instrument in Europe. During the Seven Years' War this tiny state, with only a subvention from Britain, held off the mighty empires of Austria, France, and Russia.

Efficiency and Despotism

There was no independent municipal life in Prussia, since urban areas were subject to the same central administrative controls as the rest of the kingdom. However, there were patent rewards for submitting to this despotism. The sanitation in the towns was exemplary; religious toleration was a reality; and the requirements of manufacturers were sufficiently respected to allow them to break through the restrictions imposed by the old guilds and corporations.

It has been maintained that eighteenth-century Prussia

could not have survived among the great powers, much less extended its hegemony, without the imposition of this harsh administrative system. Such bureaucratic uniformities were clearly unnecessary for the growth of Britain with its common nationality on a compact island. Keeping united the dispersed pieces of the Prussian state scattered over Germany—tiny territorial enclaves and greater areas bordering on Russia, Poland, Austria, Sweden, Saxony—was no mean task. Prussia did not even have a body of law for all her parts until the end of the century. Be that as it may, the emergence of Prussia in the eighteenth century created a new state prototype in Europe, a state with a drillmaster administration based on principles of unquestioning obedience and total regimentation, directed toward the development of unbridled and unlimited military power. This view of man and the state was later imposed upon the whole of Germany, and in our time at one critical moment threatened to engulf the continent.

CHAPTER VIII

Russia: The Servile State

AFTER the death of Peter the Great in 1725, the Russian nobles reacted with violence against his centralizing governmental system. Peter had sought to transform them into servants of the state whose preferment would depend upon their badge of service rather than upon their ancient lineage. The aristocratic revolt against the monarchy in eighteenth-century Russia assumed more bloody and sinister forms than the parallel movement in France. In Russia there were palace intrigues, cabals among the boyars, tsars assassinated. An aroused nobility recouped its traditional powers under the reign of weak and dissolute monarchs. By the time Catherine acceded to the throne in 1762, the Tsarina was no longer the scourge of the nobility but their representative, the first among the peers in the Kremlin. The noble countermovement against tsarist absolutism had been successful in large measure.

The eighteenth century has been aptly called the golden age of the Russian nobility. Concretely, the phrase meant the organization of a servile state and the extension of the absolute powers of the nobility over millions of peasants who had previously remained outside their jurisdiction. Serfdom reached its zenith during the period, at a time when in western Europe there was a general trend toward emancipation. At the same time that the nobles were being granted a greater number of privileges than they had previously enjoyed, they were being absolved from obligations which had been imposed upon them by Peter the Great. In 1762 an imperial manifesto conceded to them the right to serve the state or not at their own will, except in times of public emergency. In 1785 a Nobles' Charter confirmed and extended their various privileges. The nobility were loyal to Catherine II as a symbol of the empire, but they supported her only because she frankly and explicitly considered herself a representative of their class.

Serfs on the Manor and on the Tsar's Domains

The nobles had absolute power on their own estates. Villagers attached to a lord obeyed the orders of his steward and labored under conditions not fundamentally dissimilar from those of Roman slaves in the country villas, despite a somewhat different status in law. The servile peasant or the servile worker in the courtyard of the manor house could utilize a portion of his time for self-employment, but such earnings had also been permitted to many Roman slaves. The legal protection vouchsafed the person of the Russian serf by the Tsarina's reform decrees was nominal. There is only a handful of recorded cases when a servile peasant could and did manage to appeal to Catherine's justice over the head of a noble. Murder and brigandage committed by peasants were traditionally reserved for trial in state courts, but the judgment of most offenses committed on a noble estate was held in the manor court, where cruel corporal punishments and exile to Siberia were carelessly meted out. There was no effective sanction against the abusive treatment of serfs, even their torture unto death, at the hands of the lord of the manor.

To the peasant, his noble master was the source of all authority and beyond its bounds he knew nothing. In general practice, serfs usually were attached to the soil after the manner of western European mediaeval serfdom and were transferred to a new lord when land was alienated; but serfs could be sold off the estate, either alone or along with members of their family, depending upon the will of the lord. During the course of the latter half of the century, the peasant's dues were doubled when commuted into money payments. Servile labor varied from about three days a week to total servitude on the estate. Manumission was not unheard of, but usually it was the sick and the aged serfs who were liberated to beggary and death.

As mining and manufacturing enterprises were established, the serfs employed in these industries were organized under a work system almost identical with slave labor in the Roman mines. The Russian state had no consistent policy about the purchase of serfs by industrial entrepreneurs of the merchant class. While Peter the Great had allowed the practice, the privilege was subsequently abrogated, then renewed and modified a number of times. No disparagement was attached to the fact that a noble, through his deputy, was in control of a mining or a manufacturing enterprise, and many aristocrats operated mines, workshops, and smelters on their own estates. The contemporary western European conflict between the nobility and the *bourgeoisie* was only embryonic in Russia. Whatever industry there was tended to be devoted primarily to the manufacture of goods for the direct war purchasing order of the state or for the luxury demands of the crown. At one point Russia had exported pig iron, copper, linen, and tobacco to the markets of Europe. Even after Russian goods had been pushed out by British competition, however, they still had an assured domestic market, and the industrial units tended to be large. Often the mills and factories were controlled by noble favorites such as Catherine's lover Potemkin.

The number of peasants belonging to a given lord varied greatly, from a few handfuls on tiny holdings to great armies of more than 80,000 "souls." While in 1762 half a million peasants were still registered as freeholders, there was a growing tendency to assimilate them with state peasants, serfs attached to the tsar's domains, through the imposition of onerous dues and taxes. Within narrow limits the state peasants exercised certain functions of self-government in their villages, but in general the powers and practices of officials of the central government who supervised agglomerations of state peasants were no different from those of the stewards on proprietary estates.

Extension of Serfdom

During the course of the century secularization of church lands converted about 2,000,000 former ecclesiastical serfs into state peasants who paid money dues. Simultaneously about an equal number of state peasants were delivered into proprietary bondage by Tsarina Catherine and Tsar Paul I through land grants to their noble friends. As the Tsarina pushed the frontiers of Muscovite Russia to the southeast the system of serfdom was further extended. It is estimated that by the end of the century 19,500,000 "souls" were bondaged on noble estates and 14,500,000 "souls" were state peasants, comprising a total of 34,000,000 in a servile state out of a population of 36,000,000. In France the monarchy

was constrained to support its nobility by the multiplication of pensions and the emoluments of honorific offices;
in Russia the state peasants and the land they tilled were
the only coin of the realm available to the central government in quantity for distribution as rewards.

This extension of serfdom was not accomplished without
a series of sporadic revolts both among the serfs of proprietary estates and the peasants in the state-owned mines
and lands. Droves of peasants fled to the steppe to escape
servitude and were hunted like wild game. The culmination
of these outbursts was Pugachev's uprising in 1773, the last
great peasant rebellion. Throughout the empire a vast social
war of the lower classes was unloosed. Pugachev was a Cossack leader who declared himself tsar and roused a movement in which were intermingled the resentments of the
Don Cossack tribesmen against the incursions of the government from Moscow into the territory to which they had
migrated on the Kuban, the Terek, and the Ural, and the
grievances of the peasants throughout eastern Russia against
the added burdens of serfdom being imposed upon them.
At first the imperial forces which moved against Pugachev
were routed in pitched battles. The families of landed pro-
prietors were slaughtered and their estates ravaged by the
serfs. But these early victories were followed by an imperial vengeance which repressed the rebels with a wild
fury. Recollections of these encounters lingered in the
memory of the Russian peasantry for generations.

The Façade of Reform

In the early reformist years of her reign, Catherine's approach to Russian problems was naive. She believed that
a large population was central to the prosperity of her em-

pire, and in typical eighteenth-century fashion, she longed
to bring about the desirable increase by salutary decrees:

Russia is not only *greatly* deficient in the *number* of her Inhabitants; but at the same Time, extends her Dominion over *im-
mense* Tracts of Land; which are neither peopled nor improved.
And therefore, in a Country so circumstanced, *too much* Encouragement can never be given to the *Propagation* of the
human Species. The Peasants generally have twelve, fifteen, and
even twenty Children by one Marriage; but it rarely happens,
that one *Fourth* of these ever attains to the *Age* of Maturity.
There must therefore be some Fault, either in their Nourriture,
in their Way of Living, or Method of Education, which occasions this *prodigious* Loss and disappoints the *Hopes* of the
Empire. How flourishing would the State of this Empire be, if
we could but ward off, or *prevent* this fatal Evil by proper
Regulations! [1]

The passion for promulgating evils out of existence and
inaugurating the reign of reason by drafting beneficent
laws persisted throughout her reign. In 1767 Catherine had
assembled a commission representing various social classes
to draft a code of laws for all of Russia, on the basis of an
imperial *Instruction* into which she had poured many clichés
drawn from her reading in Montesquieu's *Spirit of the Laws*
(1748) and the Italian penologist Cesare Beccaria's *On
Crimes and Punishments* (1764). When Catherine's instruc-
tions said: "The Equality of the Citizens consists in this; that
they should be subject to the same Laws," she was prating the
standard verbiage of the philosophical moderates. She continued:

[1] William Fiddian Reddaway, ed., *Documents of Catherine the
Great; the Correspondence with Voltaire and the Instruction of
1767, in the English Text of 1768* (Cambridge [Eng.], 1931), chap.
xii, nos. 265–266, p. 257.

General or political Liberty does not consist in that licentious Notion, *That a Man may do whatever he pleases.* In a State or Assemblage of People that live together in a Community, where there are Laws, Liberty can only consist *in doing that which every One ought to do,* and *not to be constrained to do that which One ought not to do.* . . . . Liberty is the Right of doing whatsoever the Laws allow.[2]

This splendid venture earned her the plaudits of the French intellectuals, who called her a great *"législatrice"* and "star of the north." The abstractions of the *Instruction* remained dead letters, as alien to the realities of Russia as the décor of Versailles in the ancient Muscovite capital. Both were modish imitations of the French.

The Russian administrative system remained loose and chaotic, despite some departmental reorganization at its center. Local officials were not carefully supervised or checked, and peculation was rampant. It has been estimated that barely a third of the vast tax collections ever reached the imperial treasury. In this respect as in most others, the "enlightenment" of Catherine's regime was a figment of the credulity of the western European *philosophes.*

[2] *Ibid.,* chap. v, nos. 34, 36–38, p. 219.

CHAPTER IX

Balance of Power in War and Peace

EUROPE forms a political system in which the Nations inhabiting this part of the world are bound together by their relations and various interests into a single body. It is no longer, as in former times, a confused heap of detached parts, each of which had but little concern for the lot of the others, and rarely troubled itself over what did not immediately affect it. The constant attention of sovereigns to all that goes on, the custom of resident ministers, the continual negotiations that take place, make of modern Europe a sort of Republic, whose members—each independent, but all bound together by a common interest —unite for the maintenance of order and the preservation of liberty. This is what has given rise to the well-known principle of the balance of power, by which is meant an arrangement of affairs so that no State shall be in a position to have absolute mastery and dominate over the others.[1]

This definition by the Swiss jurist Emeric de Vattel, who was overimpressed with the unique interrelatedness of the powers in his own age, is the most commonly quoted eighteenth-century formulation of the principle—not the practice—of the balance of power system.

[1] Emeric de Vattel, *The Law of Nations, or the Principles of Natural Law Applied to the Conduct and to the Affairs of Nations and of Sovereigns.* A translation of the 1758 edition (Washington, 1916), p. 251.

Machiavelli had come close to the idea of a balance of power in his political theory; the doctrine had been practiced by states and empires for thousands of years before him; but not until the eighteenth century was the term in general use, with full awareness of its implications, in all the chancelleries of Europe. The English phrase and its French equivalent, *équilibre européen,* first became current about 1700.

The concept of a "balance" was derived from the language of the physicist, whose discoveries had had so powerful an impact on European consciousness. As royal ministers discoursed on a system of the balance of power among the chief nations of the continent, they reasoned in a manner which they believed to accord with good scientific method and principles. They marshaled a set of facts about the expanding or contracting economies, the resources, and the military intentions of the various states, and then drew deductions which became the point of departure for their own national policy. The political advisers of the great monarchs discussed alliances and alignments as if these "combinations," as they called them, were chemical formulae. The whole vocabulary of international politics was an adaptation from the materialist philosophy and scientific language of the age. In 1773, for example, the Duc de Broglie, secret agent of the king, presented the dying Louis XV with a memorandum which purported to be a realistic summation of all the elements involved in the European balance of power. He entitled his memorial: *Reasoned hypotheses on the present position of France in the political system of Europe and conversely the position of Europe with respect to France. Finally, the new combinations which should or might result from the various relationships in the political system of*

Europe. The study was prefaced with the maxim: "No effects without causes."

The new diplomacy took for granted that the self-interest of the kingdom and "reason of state" were unquestioned absolutes. Even when monarchs gave justifications for their declarations of war they rarely claimed that they were fighting for the triumph of a religious or moral principle. A state frankly sought preponderance over its neighbors, whom it purposed to outweigh in the naked struggle of power politics. There were no abstract ideals for which nations went to war and men perished.

Upsetting the Balance of Power

The balance of political power, like any physical balance, was a delicate equilibrium of opposing or rival forces, dependent on their strength remaining relatively equal. The conception was a static one, in harmony with the eighteenth-century view of a mechanical universe. All the elements in the European political system were, like atomic weights, absolute and finite. Ideally they had to be so arranged on the scale of power that they created a state of equilibrium known as peace. If there was imbalance resulting from change, there had to be a restoration of the ideal order by a rearrangement of the weights on both sides of the scale.

This balance of power was precarious. It was in constant danger of being upset by a monarch's dying without issue, which immediately set the powers into agitated motion to gain possession of the vacant throne; by a marriage among royal families which unduly strengthened one power; by the accession to the throne of a great empire of a woman or of a madman, revealing obvious signs of frailty in a state and whetting the appetites of its neighbors; or by the emergence of a monarch blunt and voracious who was possessed by the ambition to win glory and power through war and did not give a fig for the whole European equilibrium.

If any state was in the process of becoming enlarged too quickly at the expense of weak members—Russia extending herself into Turkey and Poland, for example—the other powers had to be appeased by being given a share in the booty. Feeble Poland was declared to be a danger to the European equilibrium because it was in a state of anarchy and a temptation to its aggressive neighbors. This was the theoretical justification for the infamous Partition of Poland in 1772. The balance of power was a principle of peace as long as there were readily available territories for the great dynasts to divide or exchange by arrangement. But when, in the name of balance of power, covetous hands were raised to grab the lands of a neighbor who had waxed too fat, war was the likely outcome of the encroachment. Such wars, waged for specific territorial objectives, were usually concluded, however, before a combatant reached the point of utter defeat which would have spelled unconditional surrender. Thus there was opportunity for negotiation, and a formula would be devised in accordance with which a juggling of the status of satellite areas and dependencies of the great powers recompensed them in one part of Europe for military losses in another. Sometimes the two armies fought each other to a standstill, then withdrew, reserving a decisive test of strength for another occasion. The Peace of Aix-la-Chapelle in 1748, at which both sides, the British and the French, restored their colonial conquests to the *status quo ante bellum*, was typical enough of the outcome of armed contests in the first half of the century.

Foreign Intelligence

In the attempt of each state to evolve a rational system of foreign policy, the gathering of information about the war potential and designs of all other European powers became an important function of the ministries of foreign affairs. It was an age of secret diplomacy and the first widespread use of intelligence agents who despatched reports on morale, on economic resources, and on the key personalities in office in the rival states. Diplomacy was conducted with an intricate apparatus of codes and courier systems, presumably designed to assure secrecy. In practice, however, there were few major diplomatic maneuvers, secret treaties, or minor personal affairs of the reigning sovereigns which were not known simultaneously in all of the five great courts of Europe. Both special emissaries and official ambassadors seem to have had rather easy access to the innermost cabinets of most of the European courts to which they were accredited. In this game of kings, dynastic power politics, the gossips and the loose-tongued traitors and informers—male, female, or androgyne like the notorious Chevalier d'Eon—kept intelligence flowing constantly in all directions across the continent. The cabinet of Frederick II was something of an exception in this respect as in many others. The King was almost psychopathically suspicious, and the stringent security measures of his court helped him to achieve a few of the only real diplomatic and military surprises in the century.

Eighteenth-Century Warfare: Its Magnitude and Character

Students of the magnitude of wars have noted that in proportion to its population the Age of Reason was less bloody than the seventeenth century and not quite so pacific as the nineteenth. If the War of the Spanish Succession which ended in 1713 is attached to the seventeenth century and the coalitions against the French Revolution are reckoned to the score of the nineteenth, the picture is much more striking. It shows an unusually long period of relative peace on the European continent from the Treaty of Utrecht to the outbreak of the French Revolution.

Eighteenth-century war was literally an extension of politics, as Clausewitz later wrote, and diplomacy was the fine art of avoiding or settling wars. The wars were therefore qualitatively and quantitatively different from the conflicts of the twentieth century in which ideologies, mass armies, and novel instruments of destruction altered the fundamental character of human combat. The casualties of war in our own century have already exceeded those of the whole of the eighteenth at least tenfold, though the population has only doubled. These statistics are not very precise, but as a contemporary sociologist of war has remarked, the refined techniques of the scientific laboratory are not necessary in a butcher shop.

Eighteenth-century wars never altogether lost their chivalric aspect—as in that memorable exchange between the British and the French at Fontenoy in 1745: there is a story that the rival commanders exhorted each other with courteous protestations, "Sir, you fire first!" The brilliant maneuver of an enemy commander was appreciated as an act of virtuosity. Cruel treatment of prisoners was not general, though in this sphere too Frederick II was a conspicuous innovator, forcing prisoners of war to join his own decimated troops as replacements.

Militarism and Pacifism

Not even professional practitioners of war like the Belgian Prince Karl Joseph de Ligne (1735–1814), who had led armies for seven different nations and had exchanged witticisms with monarchs in every major court in Europe, extolled the virtues of war in twentieth-century fascist dithyrambs. What he wrote of the "noblest of the scourges" was rather characteristic of members of his class, who regarded war as a necessary periodic bleeding of the people:

Peace is a time of apathy when there is perhaps more evil than in wartime, but it is not as evident, because its course is slower. I would be the first to detest war if sickness, bad administration, hunger, an almost universal aspect of discontent, yea, of mutiny and near revolt, were not the consequence of a long peace. . . . At the end of three years of war, the army needs to rest up, especially if there have been many hard engagements and daring undertakings; but at the end of ten years of peace, the best army must inevitably decline. It is difficult to remain in the same position. . . . What does not ascend almost always declines.[2]

At the same time, there was also a strong antimilitarist trend in the age. It produced two grand projects of universal peace, one by a French moralist, the Abbé St. Pierre (1658–1743), and one by the German philosopher Immanuel

[2] Prince Karl Joseph de Ligne, *De la paix*, in *Oeuvres du Prince de Ligne*, précédées d'une introduction par Albert Lacroix (Brussels, 1860), II, 339, 341.

Kant (1724–1804). Confirmed pacifists such as the British statesman Robert Walpole (1676–1745) and the French Prime Minister Cardinal Fleury held power and kept the peace for decades. Walpole's brilliant son Horace could sardonically strip the art of war of its noble pretensions. "Every age has some ostentatious system to excuse the havoc it commits. Conquest, honour, chivalry, religion, balance of power, commerce, no matter what, mankind must bleed, and take a term for a reason." [3] Though they lived by the favor of the great monarchs, the *philosophes* loathed war and were violent in their denunciation of the "despoilers of provinces" and the "infamous thieves . . . bathed in the blood and tears of the peoples." The ideal of the useful and agreeable was beginning to compete with the glorious. The figure of the conquering hero idealized by French neo-classicism lost its enchantment for the poets of the eighteenth century. "The boast of heroism in this enlightened age," wrote Oliver Goldsmith, "is justly regarded as a qualification of a very subordinate rank, and mankind now begin to look with becoming horror on these foes to man." [4]

Recruitment of Armies

Eighteenth-century armies were recruited by hiring or impressment with or without the benefit of persuasive intoxicants. At one time the army of France had about half and Prussia a third of its men from foreign parts; only toward the end of the century was conscription more generally in-

[3] Horace Walpole to Sir Horace Mann, May 26, 1762, in Walpole's *Letters*, ed. by Mrs. Paget Toynbee (Oxford, 1904), V, 210.

[4] Oliver Goldsmith, *The Citizen of the World; or Letters of a Chinese Philosopher, Residing in London, to His Friends in the East* (1762). Quoted from the Everyman's Library edition (London, 1934), p. 105.

troduced. Of all the great states Russia alone had an army composed of native serfs. The Romanovs had no money with which to purchase troops, hence in the eighteenth century they began to throw into European battles their seemingly endless supply of peasant soldiers. Though most European army officers were natives of the state they served, key commanders in the field were often foreigners who passed from one court to another, selling their strategic and tactical skills without being considered traitors as long as they fought well for their masters of the moment. The practice of the *condottieri* had survived. Mercenary troops lacked the fervor of the national armies of the following centuries and those who died in battle were regarded not as martyrs but as soldiers who had merely succumbed to the hazards of their profession.

Since the conflicts of the century were wars of armies, not of peoples, a line of demarcation was drawn between battle among enemy troops and a general ravaging of the countryside. This sparing of civilians was less a symptom of growing humanitarianism among the enlightened despots than a consequence of the requirements of military discipline, for if the riffraff which had been impressed or hired for the armies had been allowed a measure of personal freedom, they would have disappeared among the civilian population. A few acts of pillage, because they were unusual, became engraved on the memory of mankind.

The French and Prussian Armies

After his death, the French army forged by Louis XIV steadily declined until it ceased to be the most formidable military force on the continent. It was weighted down with a superabundance of officers, for this was the chief occupation permissible to a nobility whose numbers were being regularly augmented with new creations. The appointment of marshals and general officers depended less on competence than on court intrigue at Versailles, and a fast rotation of command often paralyzed military operations in the middle of a campaign. An indifferent French nobility stood at the head of an army drawn from the dregs of society and bought in the market of mercenaries. This explains in part at least the defeat on the European battlefields of the richest and most populated state of the continent.

The outstanding military phenomenon of the century was the army of Frederick II of Prussia. His officer corps was a closely knit body of nobles endowed with special privileges and weighted with duties and obligations. Since Frederick II could not always afford to buy troops as the Bourbons and the Hapsburgs did, he sent press gangs into the weaker German states, denuding whole villages of their male population.

The iron discipline which Frederick II imposed on the Prussian army became the model for generations of military leaders. Prussian drill was the attempt to kill the nascent reasoning power and to curb the refractory spirit of the impressed soldier. It was the policy of the "Old Fritz" to make a soldier fear the enemy less than he dreaded his own officers. This, he believed, was the way to win victories out of all proportion to the number of his troops and the limited resources of his kingdom. The officers had to devote a substantial proportion of their energies to forestalling desertions from this military servitude, but an instrument of warfare was thus created which, because it was used with signal success, was emulated by other monarchs.

Status of the Powers after Utrecht

A balance of power system had been deliberately embodied in the Peace of Utrecht (1713) which ended the War of the Spanish Succession, and with minor exceptions it was maintained through negotiation and without war for about a quarter of a century thereafter. In the compromises reached by this international treaty, Philip of Bourbon, grandson of Louis XIV, was finally recognized as king of Spain, but it was explicitly set forth that the "security and liberties of Europe could by no means bear the union of the Kingdoms of France and Spain under one and the same King." On the other side of the balance, Austria was granted possession of the Spanish Netherlands, Naples, Milan, and Sardinia, a dispersed empire almost impossible to administer and defend; and England acquired strong points, islands, and colonies—Gibraltar, Minorca, Nova Scotia, Hudson Bay, and Newfoundland. The Duchy of Savoy and the Electorate of Brandenburg were elevated from their low status and recognized by the powers as kingdoms.

Europe presented the appearance of a great multiplicity of states, but until the middle of the eighteenth century there were only two major rival dynastic land powers on the continent, each with a system of satellites, the House of Bourbon and the House of Hapsburg—both Catholic Defenders of the Faith. In the early years of the century, a combination of Protestant maritime powers, the British and the Dutch, had contained the expansive monarchy of Louis XIV and by supporting the rival House of Hapsburg had prevented him from possessing the continent.

In the second half of the century, the situation in Europe was complicated by the appearance of two new forces of magnitude in the east, Russia and Prussia. The Russian Empire, a great sprawling land mass, began to achieve a measure of centralized state organization akin to that of the western powers, and concomitantly it acquired vast new territories by penetrating toward the south and the southeast, gobbling away great chunks from the Mohammedan powers of Turkey and Persia and creating new frontiers. Once the Russian flank was protected in the west by the Partition of Poland, this dynamic imperialism seized huge areas whose significance was hardly recognized at the time. The Treaty of Küchük Kainarja (1774) opened the Black Sea, the Bosporus, and the Dardanelles to the hitherto landlocked empire. Russia on the Adriatic and Russia in Constantinople became the next goals of this persistent drive.

With Frederick II, a monarch came to the throne of Prussia who had appropriately masked his political philosophy in a treatise entitled *Anti-Machiavel*, of which Voltaire in his *Memoirs* remarked with superb insight: "If Machiavelli had had a prince for disciple, the first thing he would have advised him to do would have been to write against Machiavelli." [5] Frederick's passion for strategic aggrandizement, his aggressions against the House of Hapsburg and small German states, were major factors in upsetting the eighteenth-century balance of power. They were the immediate causes of the bloodiest wars of the age.

Spain, Holland, and Sweden, great powers in the seventeenth century, were now in eclipse. England sent her pounds sterling into the European wars, but committed only

[5] François Marie Arouet de Voltaire, *Mémoires de M. de Voltaire écrits par lui-même* (Paris, 1886), p. 19.

a small number of men. Her attention had already become focused upon the overseas empire.

Diplomatic Revolution in Mid-Century

As a consequence of the emergence of Prussia, about the middle of the century a great diplomatic revolution occurred on the continent. In 1740, when Frederick marched against Austria (War of the Austrian Succession), the French had made common cause with him. England had ranged itself by the side of the young Empress, sending money and ships to harass France and right the balance of opposing forces. In 1756 France abruptly switched from support of Prussia, which could grow only at Austrian expense, to a full-blown defensive and offensive alliance with the traditional Hapsburg enemy. The marriage of Marie Antoinette, daughter of Maria Theresa, to the future king of France was to become the dynastic symbol of the union. The Austrian ambassador to France, Prince von Kaunitz, had been the pivotal figure in effecting the realignment of Europe. It was a diplomatic somersault of great moment: the two land empires, ancient rivals for the supremacy of the continent, hard pressed by two expansive kingdoms, the British and the Prussians, who had once been their clients, resolved to change their "political systems," in the language of the chancelleries. The Duc de Broglie, in his secret memorial to the King in 1773, denounced the Austrian orientation as the primary cause of French military decline. He believed that the Alliance of 1756 had brought an emphasis on land rather than on maritime war, with the result that "by an incredible displacement France seems to have lost her rank at the head of the great powers."

The Seven Years' War on the Continent

Frederick II of Prussia challenged the Bourbon-Hapsburg alliance with a flagrant breach of international mores, the invasion of Saxony without warning in September 1756—the opening thrust of the Seven Years' War. The great continental powers resolved to crush the upstart violator who had eschewed the formalities of law and the customs of the Holy Roman Empire to which he belonged. Frederick was literally encircled by Russia, Sweden, France, and Austria. It was England who came to the rescue of the Hohenzollern, as had France earlier in the century, and thus helped forge the state which less than 200 years later brought her to the edge of the abyss. England used the instruments of religious propaganda to rouse sympathy for the Protestant monarchy of Prussia and sent heavy subsidies, notwithstanding King George II's description of Frederick as a "mischievous rascal . . . the most dangerous and ill-disposed prince in Europe."

In succoring the Prussians, England was proceeding in accordance with her general "political system," a system of strategy whose lodestar was France. To checkmate France, distract her on the continent by feeding the military ambitions of her enemies, and thus handicap her in the struggle for overseas colonies, was for eighteenth-century Britain the path to commercial supremacy. British pounds helped to keep the Prussian army in the field despite severe losses and such crushing defeats that Frederick at one desperate moment contemplated suicide. After years of indecisive combat Frederick's grim tenacity and extraordinary military genius, plus the withdrawal of Russia, compelled Austria to sue for peace, though the bedraggled remnants of the Prussian forces hardly resembled a victorious army.

In the meantime, with the European war prolonged and France heavily engaged, England had a chance to administer the final coup to her rival on the continents of Asia and America.

Colonial Warfare between France and England

On the sea lanes to the world outside of Europe and on the frontiers of colonial settlements, the contest between England and France in alliance with Spain had continued virtually throughout the century. The colonial wars were waged for the right to trade with the new settlements, for the possession of treasure and fertile soil, and for the promise of long future exploitation. The fighting was not always characterized by the charming battle manners of some European engagements. In North America the settlers and mercenaries on both sides hired Indian savages whom they stimulated with the rival firewaters of the European contenders. (In the final reckoning, the British rum won over the French brandy.) The long-drawn-out skirmishes neither began with formal declarations nor were they ended by the treaties of peace, though the fiercest encounters tended to coincide with the renewal of warfare in Europe. The conflict ceased only when one of the participants had been totally eliminated.

In 1738 the representatives of the merchant class in the British Parliament, impatient to break the Franco-Spanish monopoly of trade with South America and bitter over Spanish search of British ships for contraband, were roused to white fury by a Captain Jenkins who told of his mutilation at the hands of the Spaniards—he actually exhibited a cut-off ear. Prime Minister Robert Walpole, reluctantly breaking a long period of peace with the Bourbons of France and Spain, launched the War of Jenkins' Ear, which lasted for about a decade, a counterpart to the War of the Austrian Succession in Europe and similarly inconclusive. Again, during the Seven Years' War (1756–1763) on the continent, when French military resources were heavily committed against Frederick, the overseas struggle between France and Britain was rekindled with new violence (the French and Indian War). After a long series of colonial affrays, peace in 1763 found England in possession of Canada and India—substantial recompense for the gallant captain's disfigurement.

The final outcome of the colonial struggle revealed profound differences in the British and French constitutions, even as it was prophetic of the realignment of great powers in the next century. France and Britain had each chosen to develop the military arm best suited to the national interest as interpreted by the most vocal elements in the state. In Britain, dominated by rich merchants and landowners, there was universal recognition that commerce was the source of the nation's wealth, and there was a Parliament where colonial interests could obtain a hearing. Protected by the Channel from continental armies, Britain poured her strength into the building of a merchant marine and a navy which could protect the trade with her colonial settlements and could carry them effective military aid at times of crisis.

It was otherwise with the French colonial settlements and the merchants who stood to profit from the overseas trade. Without an assembly where they could present their needs, their future rested upon the vicissitudes of court favor. Hostile voices were raised against them. The nobility, eating up the substance of the state in pensions, resented and ridiculed expenditures on what they considered the barren wastelands of North America. The middle-class intellectuals were too preoccupied with their crusade for religious and governmental reform to concern themselves with the outposts of empire. Voltaire paraded his indifference: "You know," he wrote, "these two nations [England and France] are at war for a few acres of snow in Canada, and that they are spending more on this fine war than all Canada is worth. It is beyond my poor capacity to tell you whether there are more madmen in one country than in the other. . . ." [6] The French mercantilists, too, cared nothing for Canada, because it supplied no new products for the realm.

Underestimating the colonial possessions, the French made the occupation of more land in Europe the goal of their military policy and dedicated their resources to maintaining an army for continental warfare. The defense of the empire was given only secondary consideration, and the great navy built by Louis XIV was allowed to decline until it became nothing more than a fleet of privateers harassing Britain's commerce with her colonies; by the second half of the century it no longer played a vital role in protecting the prestige and power of France. Without adequate military and financial support from the mother country, the neglected colonies in Asia and the New World inevitably slipped from French control.

Consequences of the Seven Years' War

Though Europe had been profusely bled, its political boundaries were only slightly altered by the Treaty of Hu-

[6] François Marie Arouet de Voltaire, *Candide, or Optimism* (1759), tr. by Richard Aldington (London, 1939), p. 109.

bertusburg (1763) between Austria and Prussia; the changes on other continental land masses, embodied in the Treaty of Paris of the same year, were, however, momentous.

England's support of the Prussian soldier-king's lawless rampage had paid munificent dividends. The French had been ousted from India, where English hegemony was now assured. Canada passed from French to English hands, Spain gave up Florida, and the French were evicted from their posts along the Ohio, removing the obstacle to westward expansion by the British colonists. Senegal, too, with its profitable West African slave trade, became a British prize. In short, Britain emerged from the Seven Years' War the preponderant maritime and colonial power in the world.

The new British colonial empire had been bought for a song. On the battlefield of Plassey in 1757, where the French were virtually eliminated from India, the British general Robert Clive commanded 3,000 men, of whom 900 were Europeans, and of these only 20 men fell. William Pitt, the Great Commoner who directed the war, estimated that Canada was won with 1,500 lives. In contrast with England, the cost of the war to Prussia was enormous. Its total population of about 4,500,000 was diminished by 500,000, Frederick wrote, and the war devastation in Brandenburg resembled the continental ravages of the previous century rather than contemporary battlefields. While Britain acquired whole continents beyond the seas, Frederick was merely secured in his possession of Silesia, snatched some twenty years before.

"What did France lose? The world, nothing more!" [7] was the bitter lament of her nineteenth-century nationalist

[7] Jules Michelet, *Histoire de France au dix-huitième siècle* (Paris, 1867), p. 123.

historian Michelet. Of a once-mighty empire, she now retained only two islands off Newfoundland and fishing rights
in the St. Lawrence, in addition to some West Indian islands
valuable for their sugar and other exotic crops. But the
French monarchy, not perceiving the historic worth of its
vast colonial losses, was unable to sense the depth of hu-
miliation to which it had sunk at the Peace of Paris. Indeed,
the Duc de Choiseul thought he had turned a shrewd diplomatic trick when he exchanged Canada for the Antilles,
which had been captured by the English during the war
and which they relinquished the more readily to appease
British West Indian interests fearful of the competition of
cheaper French West Indian sugar within the British Empire. Colonial power had become the monopoly of England.
The Seven Years' War left France the mere continental
state which she has remained ever since, despite feverish
nineteenth-century attempts to rebuild the semblance of an
empire.

Territorial Changes, 1714-1783

During the century, the continental states had jostled
one another for position, trying to gain possession of the
greatest possible extent of territory, exchanging bits of land
here and there, perpetrating sneak invasions when a neighbor was engaged on another front, cannibalizing the weak.
Though the European boundaries of dynastic states were
altered, the reapportionment of lands was effected with only
one full-scale blood-letting, the Seven Years' War. In summary, these are the major territorial reallocations which
occurred in Europe from the Peace of Utrecht to the Treaty
of Paris in 1783: France acquired the Duchy of Lorraine;

Prussia was swollen with accretions from Poland and the Silesia of the Hapsburgs; Russia ate away large segments of the Turkish Empire; Austria won principalities in northern Italy and the Balkans; the Bourbons of Spain wrested the Kingdom of the Two Sicilies from Austria; Poland was torn apart by her three neighbors; France was restored the right of fortifying Dunkirk; and Minorca was returned to Spain.

The underlying mechanism of the balance of power in Europe had worked after a fashion, resulting in a series of coalitions against any one state which appeared on the verge of achieving marked preponderance. Europe had united against the France of Louis XIV; then, in the War for the Austrian Succession, the powers pounced on the Hapsburgs, who had acquired 4,000 square miles in the treaties of Rastadt (1714) and Passarowitz (1718); then on Prussia in the Seven Years' War. A similar maneuver was perpetrated against Britain during the War for American Independence. Each time, in the process of creating a grand alliance and triumphing over the adversary, a new power, a member of the alliance, would emerge swollen with victories. In its turn, the dominant state had to be humbled by another alignment. The victory of the grand alliance in the war for American Independence—the defeat of England by a combination of the American colonials, the Dutch, the French, and the Spanish, supported by the menacing neutrality of Russia—led political commentators to declare that England, too, had met its nemesis and was entering a decline. At the moment when the French monarchy was overtaken by the great Revolution of 1789, her agents were plotting, rather lamely, to be sure, a descent on England and the renewal of a full-scale attack in India.

The American Revolution

The American Revolution has a many-sided significance in the history of the eighteenth century, apart from its role in balance-of-power politics. It may be considered as a War of Independence, in which rising nationalist forces on a new continent threw off the mother country's yoke and proclaimed the existence of a sovereign people. As a struggle for liberation it was the predecessor of a long line of nationalist revolutions in Europe and South America against the major dynastic states.

It also spelled the end of the simple mercantilist policy in accordance with which a mother country exploited colonies solely for her own economic benefit, prohibiting them from developing native industries which might be competitive with her own and restricting the growth of their commerce in order to expand her own merchant marine. The imposition of Navigation Acts governing American trade, the levying of irksome taxes, and a feint at the strict enforcement of these unpopular measures were futile attempts to carry out a policy of penalizing productive colonial pioneers for the benefit of British industrial and commercial lobbies who had access to the officers of the crown. After the defeat of France in 1763, the colonists no longer feared invasion from Canada and they could dispense with that protective service which the mother country had once provided. Though at first they rebelled only against the regulation of their economy by a government in which they had no direct representation, they soon came to question the worth of any tie with a remote land across the sea.

Far more momentous than the skirmishes, small battles, and protracted sieges of the Revolutionary War was the intellectual contagion of the revolutionary spirit generated in America. The American Revolution was led by men who had been nurtured on the writings of Locke, Montesquieu, and Rousseau. Meeting at Philadelphia on July 4, 1776, they proclaimed "a decent respect to the opinions of mankind" and announced the social contract theory of the European political philosophers as the official policy of their new federation. Moreover, they proceeded to act upon this social contract theory, which, as expounded in Locke's *Second Treatise on Civil Government* (1690) and Rousseau's *Social Contract* (1762), had justified the right of revolution against tyrants. In a Declaration of Independence they dissolved the contract with their sovereign in a rational, formal manner, meticulously listing their grievances. What is more amazing, they succeeded in maintaining their principles against the greatest maritime power in the world. The right of revolution was put into actual practice. It is one of the ironies of history that the continental autocrats, in their zeal to humble Britain, were the prime sustainers of these American rebels.

The success of the American Revolution exerted an immediate and significant ideological influence on Europe. In France, one of the parties of government reform called itself "*les américains,*" and the language of American state constitutions reverberates in the text of the Declaration of the Rights of Man adopted by the French Constituent Assembly. The Americans of the Revolution were the embodiment of the ideals of the moderates among the *philosophes*. The American was the natural man, making his way in the wilderness without a king, without an aristocracy, without a dominant clergy. He was clothed in reason and he believed in science and in productive labor. Benjamin

Franklin, the revolutionary emissary to France, was a composite of American virtues, and when he embraced the dying Voltaire at a session of the French Academy in 1778, men were moved to weep.

The American revolutionaries had derived sustenance from eighteenth-century English and French thinkers. In turn, the new union established across the Atlantic was proof for Europeans that the moral and social ideals of the Age of Reason could in fact become the foundation of a free society. In a pamphlet published anonymously in Amsterdam in 1786 entitled *Influence of the American Revolution on Europe*, the great French mathematician and philosopher Marie Jean de Condorcet (1743–1794) sensed the full import of the American experience for the Old World. It was not enough, he maintained, that the great principles of his age

be written in the books of the *philosophes* and in the hearts of virtuous men. It is necessary that the poor and ignorant man be able to read them in the example of a great people. America has given us this example. The act which declared its independence is a simple and sublime exposition of these rights so sacred and so long forgotten. . . . The spectacle of a great people where the rights of man are respected is useful to all others, despite differences of climate, of customs, and of constitutions. . . . It becomes apparent what effect the enjoyment of these rights has on general well-being. The man who has never feared an outrage on his person acquires a nobler and gentler soul; he whose property is always secure finds it easy to be honest; the citizen who is subject only to law has more patriotism and courage.[8]

[8] *Influence de la Révolution de l'Amérique sur l'Europe, par un habitant obscur de l'ancien hémisphère* (Amsterdam, 1786), pp. 13, 15.

Chronological Summary ~~~~~~~

1713	Peace of Utrecht.
1714–1727	Reign of George I, King of England.
1715	Death of Louis XIV, King of France.
1715–1774	Reign of Louis XV, King of France.
1727–1760	Reign of George II, King of England.
1733	Voltaire's *Letters Concerning the English Nation*.
1738	Outbreak of the War of Jenkins' Ear.
1740–1786	Reign of Frederick II, King of Prussia.
1740–1780	Reign of Maria Theresa of Austria.
1740–1748	War of the Austrian Succession.
1745	Battle of Fontenoy, Austrian Netherlands.
1748	Peace of Aix-la-Chapelle.
	Montesquieu's *Spirit of the Laws*.
1751–1772	The *Grande Encyclopédie*.
1756–1763	Seven Years' War.
1757	Battle of Plassey, India.
1759	Voltaire's *Candide*.
1760–1820	Reign of George III, King of England.
1762	Rousseau's *Social Contract*.
1762–1796	Reign of Catherine II, Tsarina of Russia.
1763	Treaties of Hubertusburg and Paris.
1765–1780	Coregency of Maria Theresa and Joseph II of Austria.
1765–1790	Reign of Joseph II as Holy Roman Emperor.

1767   Catherine II's *Instruction*.

1769   James Watt's steam engine.

1772   First Partition of Poland.

1773   Dissolution of the Jesuit Order.
       Pugachev's Rebellion.

1774   Treaty of Küchük Kainarja.

1774–1793   Reign of Louis XVI, King of France.

1776   Declaration of Independence.
       Adam Smith's *Enquiry into the Nature and Causes
       of the Wealth of Nations*.

1781   Joseph II's Edict of Toleration.

1781–1785   Joseph II's Edicts Emancipating the Serfs.

1783   Peace of Versailles.

1789   Convocation of the Estates-General in France.

Suggestions for Further Reading

THREE volumes of the Harper and Brothers series entitled *The Rise of Modern Europe,* under the editorship of William L. Langer, cover the period 1715 to 1789: Penfield Roberts, *The Quest for Security, 1715–1740* (New York, 1947); W. L. Dorn, *Competition for Empire, 1740–1763* (New York, 1940); Leo Gershoy, *From Despotism to Revolution, 1763–1789* (New York, 1944). The broad scope and comprehensive bibliographies of these works make them excellent starting points for further study of the period. The most recent comprehensive summary by French scholars is Roland Mousnier and Ernest Labrousse, *Le XVIIIᵉ siècle* (Paris, 1953), volume V in the *Histoire générale des civilisations* series. Volume VII of *The New Cambridge Modern History,* edited by J. O. Lindsay (Cambridge, Eng., 1957) covers the period 1713–1763.

The following is a selected list of works in English primarily on the domestic politics of the major European powers: D. Dakin, *Turgot and the Ancien Régime in France* (London, 1939); L. B. Namier, *England in the Age of the American Revolution* (London, 1930) and *The Structure of Politics at the Accession of George III* (London, 1929, 2 vols.); Basil Williams, *The Whig Ascendancy* (Oxford, 1939); S. K. Padover, *The Revolutionary Emperor: Joseph II* (New York, 1934); R. Kerner, *Bohemia in the Eighteenth Century* (New York, 1932); H. Marczali, *Hungary in the Eighteenth Century* (Cambridge,

Eng., 1910); W. H. Bruford, *Germany in the Eighteenth Century* (New York, 1935); George Peabody Gooch, *Frederick the Great* (New York, 1947); G. T. Robinson, *Rural Russia under the Old Regime* (New York, 1932).

The social structure of European states has of late been the subject of a number of original works: F. L. Ford, *Robe and Sword: The Regrouping of the French Aristocracy after Louis XIV* (Cambridge, Mass., 1953); A. Goodwin, *European Nobility in the 18th Century* (London, 1953); Elinor G. Barber, *The Bourgeoisie in 18th Century France* (Princeton, 1955); Hans Rosenberg, *Bureaucracy, Aristocracy and Autocracy: The Prussian Experience; 1660–1816* (Cambridge, Mass., 1958). R. R. Palmer, *The Age of the Democratic Revolution: A Political History of Europe and America, 1760–1800* (Princeton, 1959) is the first volume of an important synthesis underlining the similarity of apparently disparate political and institutional developments throughout the European continent and in the United States.

The Industrial Revolution in England has become the central problem of eighteenth-century economic history. The classic treatment is Paul Mantoux, *The Industrial Revolution in the Eighteenth Century*, translated by M. Vernon (London, 1935). T. S. Ashton, *The Industrial Revolution, 1760–1830* (Oxford, 1948), a recent re-examination in the Home University Library series, offers a number of provocative, if highly controversial, conclusions. The judgments of J. and B. Hammond in their *Rise of Modern Industry* (New York, 1926) have long been disputed. E. F. Heckscher, *Mercantilism* (London, 1935, 2 vols.), will remain one of the great works in the history of modern economic thought and policy. Henri Sée, *Economic and Social Conditions in France during the Eighteenth Century*, translated from the French (New York, 1927), though dated, is still useful.

The intellectual ferment of this period has been studied in

several brilliant works. Perhaps the most profound, Ernst Cassirer, *Die Philosophie der Aufklärung* (Tübingen, 1932), is now available in English (Princeton, 1951); and so is Paul Hazard, *La Pensée européenne au XVIIIe siècle* (Paris, 1946, 3 vols.), though the translation (New Haven, 1954) omits the extensive third volume of bibliographical notes. Carl L. Becker, *The Heavenly City of the Eighteenth Century Philosophers* (New Haven, 1932), remains the most thoughtful brief essay on the *philosophes;* it has been the subject of a provocative collection of papers edited by Raymond O. Rockwood, *Carl Becker's Heavenly City Revisited* (Ithaca, 1958). F. C. Green, *Minuet, A Critical Survey of French and English Literary Ideas in the Eighteenth Century* (London, 1935), is incisive. F. Hearnshaw, *The Social and Political Ideas of Some Great Thinkers of the Age of Reason* (London, 1930); Kingsley Martin, *French Liberal Thought in the Eighteenth Century* (Boston, 1929), and Daniel Mornet, *Les Origines intellectuelles de la révolution française* (3rd ed., Paris, 1938), are standard in their respective fields. The older work of Leslie Stephen, *History of English Thought in the Eighteenth Century* (New York, 1876, 2 vols.), has not been entirely superseded. Two recent general works by Americans, George Remington Havens, *The Age of Ideas, from Reaction to Revolution in Eighteenth Century France* (New York, 1955), and Lester Gilbert Crocker, *An Age of Crisis: Man and World in Eighteenth Century French Thought* (Baltimore, 1959), are of interest. Frank E. Manuel, *The Eighteenth Century Confronts the Gods* (Cambridge, Mass., 1959), presents the religious and moral problems of the age from a special viewpoint.

The work of B. Groethuysen, *Les Origines de l'esprit bourgeois en France* (Paris, 1927, 2 vols.), and of Harold J. Laski, *The Rise of European Liberalism* (New York, 1936), invite comparison for their different views of the development of the businessman's ideals. Basil Willey, *The Eighteenth Century*

Background: Studies on the Idea of Nature in the Thought of the Period (London, 1949), is an able discussion of a perennial problem. The idea of progress, first treated historically by J. B. Bury, *The Idea of Progress: An Inquiry into Its Origin and Growth* (London, 1920), has been reconsidered by Charles Frankel, *The Faith of Reason: The Idea of Progress in the French Enlightenment* (New York, 1948), and by Ronald V. Sampson, *Progress in the Age of Reason: The Seventeenth Century to the Present* (Cambridge, Mass., 1956).

A. Wolf, *A History of Science, Technology and Philosophy in the Eighteenth Century* (London, 1939), is a comprehensive reference volume.

The works of several eighteenth-century writers have been republished in popular editions: R. B. Ridman's *Portable Voltaire* (New York, 1949) and *Social Contract; Essays by Locke, Hume, and Rousseau,* with an introduction by Sir Ernest Barker (London, 1947). Everyman's Library includes in its collection works by Locke, Thomas Paine, Rousseau, Oliver Goldsmith, and Lessing; the Hafner Classics, works by Montesquieu, Hume, Adam Smith, and Rousseau. Crane Brinton, *The Portable Age of Reason Reader* (New York, 1956), presents excerpts from a wide variety of writers; Isaiah Berlin, ed., *The Age of Enlightenment* (Boston, 1956), is concentrated on philosophical texts.

Index

Absolutism, 51, 52, 53, 5, 91, 94, 106
Addison, Joseph, 41
Agriculture, 12, 14, 19, 59, 60, 64, 74, 75, 77, 83, 93, 96, 101, 103
Alembert, Jean d', 27
Alliance of 1756, 125
America, 7, 8, 21, 71, 127, 129, 132, 133, 134, 135
American Revolution, 53, 64, 76, 132-135
Amsterdam, 15, 16
Aristocracy, 2, 3, 5-7, 17, 44, 52, 54, 56, 57, 64, 71, 89, 102, 106, 134
Arkwright, Richard, 81, 82
Army, 8, 9, 19, 54-56, 64, 70, 72, 75, 88, 90, 92, 99, 100, 102, 103, 116, 118-122, 126-129
Asia, 7, 10, 11, 127, 129
Austria, 3, 11, 17, 20, 48, 86-98, 104, 105, 123, 125, 126, 130, 132
Austro-Hungarian Empire, 86-98

Bacon, Francis, 27, 29, 30
Bakewell, Robert, 78
Balance of power, 9, 11, 113-135
Balkans, 89, 132
Beccaria, Cesare, 111
Berlin, 15, 16, 18
Blackstone, William, 73
Bohemia, 87, 88, 91, 92, 95
Boulton, Matthew, 77, 80
Bourbon, 6, 7, 16, 122, 123, 126, 128, 132
Bourgeoisie, 5, 6, 32, 56, 62-68, 108

Boyle, Robert, 25
Bridgewater, Duke of, 77
Broglie, Duc de, 114, 125
Bureaucracy, 4, 6, 15, 50, 53, 73, 99, 101-103, 105
Byzantine Empire, 15

Cagliostro, 19
Canada, 128-131, 133
Capitalism, 68
Cartwright, Edmund, 81
Casanova, 19
Catherine II of Russia, 3, 17, 18, 20, 106-107, 109, 110, 111, 112
Catholic, 20, 32, 91, 95, 97
Charles VI, 86, 87
Charles Albert, 87
Chateaubriand, 65
Choiseul, Duc de, 17, 131
Christianity, 31-33, 37, 38
Church, 2, 3, 6, 7, 15, 16, 24-34, 47, 48, 57, 64, 72, 91, 93-96, 109
Cities, 11-16, 62, 63, 96
Clausewitz, 118
Clergy, 2, 3, 54, 71, 75, 134
Clive, Robert, 130
Colonies, 7, 8, 10, 19, 21, 63, 76, 81, 85, 116, 126, 127, 128, 129, 130-135
Commons, House of, 70, 71
Compte Rendu, 67
Condillac, Etienne de, 31
Condorcet, Marie Jean de, 135
Constantinople, 15, 124
Cort, Henry, 79, 80

Crime and punishment, 3, 19, 32, 46, 47, 56, 92, 96, 107
Crompton, Samuel, 82

Darby, Abraham, 79
Declaration of Independence, 36, 40, 134
Defoe, Daniel, 71
Descartes, René, 27, 28
Diderot, Denis, 18, 27, 28, 30, 60
Diplomacy, 21, 115, 117, 118, 125
Dissenters, 72

Edict of Toleration, 95
Education, 93, 97
Elizabeth of Russia, 17
Enclosures, 12
Encyclopédie, 27, 60
England, 5-7, 10-13, 16-19, 24, 30, 48, 60, 68, 69-85, 104, 105, 116, 123-135
Enlightened despots, 3-7, 47, 48, 97, 121
Enlightenment, 1, 20, 91, 97
Estates-General, 52, 54, 57

Factory system, 82-84
Feudal, 2, 3, 5, 9, 52, 89, 91, 101
Fielding, Henry, 73, 74
Fleury, Cardinal, 17, 50, 120
France, 5, 6, 7, 10, 11, 13, 16-18, 20, 21, 26, 48-68, 72, 85, 87, 101-104, 106, 109, 114, 116, 120-123, 125, 126-135
Franklin, Benjamin, 134-135
Frederick II of Prussia, 3, 17, 18, 34, 88, 90-94, 99-105, 117, 119, 122, 124-128, 130
Frederick William I of Prussia, 16
French and Indian War, 128
French Revolution, 1, 6, 7, 21, 34, 46, 57, 61, 62, 64-66, 118, 132

George II, 126
Georges of Hanover, 16, 18
Germany, 9, 11, 14, 15, 20, 24, 85, 87, 93, 105
God, 25, 26, 31-33, 36, 38, 50
Goethe, 14, 18, 38

Goldsmith, Oliver, 18, 120
Grimm, 18

Hapsburg, 7, 11, 15, 16, 19, 86-93, 95, 122-126, 132
Hargreaves, James, 82
Haugwitz, Chancellor Count Friedrich Wilhelm, 17, 89
Helvétius, Claude, 39
History, 7, 40, 101, 133, 134
Hobbes, Thomas, 42
Hohenzollern, 16, 126
Holbach, Baron d', 65
Holkham, Coke of, 78
Holland, 20, 124, 132
Holy Roman Emperor, Empire, 9, 16, 86, 87, 126
Humanitarianism, 42, 121
Hume, David, 4, 24
Hungary, 11, 86, 88, 89, 92, 94, 95

India, 8, 130, 132
Industrial Revolution, 12, 60, 72, 74, 78, 81, 82, 83
Industrial workers, 12, 59, 84
Intendants, 50, 51, 55, 56, 68
Inventions, 39, 60, 74, 75, 77, 78, 79, 81, 82
Italy, 9, 16, 18, 85, 132

Jenkins, Captain, 127
Jesuit, 20, 34, 93
Jews, 20, 95, 97
Johnson, Samuel, 75
Joseph II of Austria, 3, 16, 86, 91, 93, 94-98
Junkers, 102

Kant, Immanuel, 119-120
Kaunitz, Prince von, 17, 125
Kay, John, 81

La Mettrie, Julien de, 100-101
Laws of nature, 26, 32, 38, 45
Leibnitz, 24
Lettres de cachet, 52
Ligne, Prince Karl Joseph de, 119
Locke, John, 27, 30, 31, 134
Lombe, Thomas, 81

London, 12, 14-16, 73
Lords, House of, 71
Louis XIV, 6, 49, 51, 55, 57, 60, 99,
    121, 123, 129, 132
Louis XV, 16, 17, 49, 50-53, 114
Louis XVI, 16, 50, 52, 54

Machiavelli, 114, 124
Marie Antoinette, 125
Marie Theresa, 16, 86, 87-93, 125
Michelet, Jules, 131
Middle Ages, 3, 10, 43, 68
Migration, 11, 18, 19, 20
Monarchy, 2, 3, 4, 5, 6, 11, 15, 17,
    44, 49, 50-52, 54, 57, 68, 72, 93,
    98, 101, 106, 109, 126, 131, 132
Montesquieu, Baron de, 69, 111,
    134
Moscow, 15, 16, 110

National debt, 53, 72
Nationalism, 21
Navigation Acts, 133
Navy, 70, 72, 75, 128, 129
Necker, 66-68
Newton, Isaac, 23, 24, 25, 27, 30
Nobility, 2-7, 17, 32, 49, 52, 54-57,
    59, 62-69, 71, 77, 87, 88, 89, 91, 92,
    96, 102, 106-110, 122, 128
Nonconformist, 72

Ottoman Empire, 89; *see also* Tur-
    key

Parlement, 50-52, 55-57
Parliament, 12, 52, 67, 69, 70, 71, 73,
    127, 128
Paul I of Russia, 109
Peasants, 3, 5, 13, 21, 56, 58, 59, 62,
    66, 67, 70, 90, 91, 92, 95, 96, 102,
    103, 106-111
Peking, 16
Peter the Great, 15, 17, 106, 107, 108
Philip of Bourbon, 123
Philosophes, 6, 18, 26-31, 36, 38, 39,
    44-48, 112, 120, 134, 135
Physiocrats, 13, 43, 94
Pitt, William, 130
Plassey, battle of, 130

Poland, 20, 89, 105, 116, 124, 132
Pombal, Marquis de, 17
Poor Law, 73, 83, 84
Pope, Alexander, 44
Population, 9-15, 60, 84, 87, 110,
    118, 121, 122, 130
Portugal, 20
Pragmatic Sanction, 87
Prague, 87, 92
Priestley, John, 76
Privilege, 52, 53, 55, 56, 64, 87, 88,
    89, 107, 108, 122
Progress, 1, 2, 5, 39, 44, 45
Protestant, 32, 35, 97
Prussia, 3, 7, 10, 15, 16, 20, 34, 48,
    87, 88, 91, 94, 99-105, 120, 122, 124-
    126, 130
Pugachev, 110

Reform, 3, 5, 66, 68, 86, 89, 91-95,
    107, 110, 129, 134
Religion, 1, 6, 20, 23, 25, 26, 29, 30-
    33, 36, 41, 46, 57, 93, 94, 95, 104,
    120, 126
Richelieu, Cardinal, 51
Romanticism, 33, 37
Rome, 15, 16, 93
Rousseau, Jean-Jacques, 13, 37, 38,
    134
Russia, 3, 7, 11, 15, 17, 18-20, 48, 104,
    105, 106-112, 116, 121, 124, 126,
    132

St. Petersburg, 15
St. Pierre, Bernardin de, 119
Science, 23-34, 39, 43, 134
Self-love, 41-43
Sensibility, 37
Seven Years' War, 53, 104, 126, 128,
    129, 130, 131, 132
Siberia, 19
Smith, Adam, 43
Sonnenfels, Joseph von, 93
Spain, 20, 42, 123, 124, 127, 128, 130,
    132
Sterne, Laurence, 42
Sweden, 124, 126
Switzerland, 18

Theology, 23-35
Tocqueville, Alexis de, 62
Tories, 6
Townshend, Viscount Charles, 78
Trade, 7, 56, 63, 64, 71, 72, 76, 84, 85, 103, 104, 127, 128, 133
Travel, travelers, 16, 18, 19, 20, 36, 40, 58
Treaties of Peace: Aix-la-Chapelle, 116; Hubertusburg, 129; Küçhük Kainarja, 124; Paris, 130, 131; Passarowitz, 132; Rastadt, 132; Utrecht, 1, 7, 118, 123, 131
Turgot, 66, 67, 68
Turkey, 124, 132; *see also* Ottoman Empire

Vattel, Emeric de, 113
Versailles, 14, 49, 55, 67, 112, 122
Vienna, 15, 16, 88, 89, 90, 94, 96
Voltaire, 18, 24, 27, 29, 33, 34, 38, 42, 69, 124, 129, 135

Walpole, Horace, 120
Walpole, Robert, 120, 127
War of Jenkins' Ear, 128
War of the Austrian Succession, 87, 125, 128, 132
War of the Spanish Succession, 118, 123
Warfare, 7, 104, 118, 122, 127, 129
Wars, 6, 7, 18, 25, 46, 54, 87, 88, 91, 103, 104, 115, 116, 118, 119, 121, 124, 125, 126, 127, 128, 129, 130, 131, 133
Watt, James, 77, 80
Wedgwood, Josiah, 77, 81, 83
Weimar, 14
Whately, Thomas, 72
Whigs, 6, 12, 71
Wilkes, John, 70
Wilkinson, John, 80
William III, 70

Young, Arthur, 19, 75